Computer Processing of Library Files at Durham University

An ordering and cataloguing facility for a small collection using an IBM 360/67 machine

by R. N. ODDY

Durham University Library

1971

© Durham University Library
Publication No. 7

Printed by Cherrett Brothers Ltd., Bishop Auckland
First edition 1971
sbn 900009 01 2

Late in 1967 Durham University Library was preparing
to establish a "Short Loan Collection" of books and
periodical articles in heavy demand by students. Shelved
apart from the main bookstock, although in the same
building, and on closed access, the collection would need
separate catalogues. Perhaps 5,000 items was thought to
be the likely eventual size. There seemed a need, and
an opportunity, to provide a catalogue simpler than the
existing one but at the same time capable of experimental
arrangement. Books would also need to be ordered.

A few miles away, at Newcastle University Library,
book orders and accessions lists were being handled on a
KDF 9 computer. The thought naturally occurred: could
we use modified versions of the Newcastle programs to
produce not only orders and lists but public catalogues
sorted in various ways? An additional benefit would be
the experience in automation this would give us in the
library, although the scope of the project was limited.

The Directors of the computing laboratories at
Newcastle and Durham kindly agreed to provide facilities.
Bob Oddy, who was asked to take on the investigation,
concluded that it made better sense to write new programs
for the more powerful IBM 360/67 then coming into service
on a shared basis between the two Universities than to
re-write the KDF 9 ones. The library's requirements,
when we came to formulate them more closely, contributed
to this conclusion.

We were asking not just for a catalogue or a series
of catalogues sorted in a few different ways, but for a
flexible recording, updating, sorting, selecting and
printing system which moreover would give us readily
legible and tolerably well laid out computer print-out.
At the time it didn't seem to us a heavy demand so we
called for the job to be done in six months into the
bargain. Before the time was up we were able to send
off printed orders for the books, and the Short Loan
Collection was duly inaugurated in October 1968, although
by then we had come to see the task in a more respectful
light. It was some months before computerised public
catalogues were available. When they did appear we, and
our readers, were impressed with their neat appearance,
and they did much to promote use of the collection.

iii

Once the programs had been developed to a stable
point it became necessary for Bob Oddy to write this
manual, which gives Durham University Library, the users
at present, all the information needed to operate the
system.   Believing that others might find it of interest
and possible use, we have decided to give it wider
distribution.

To some extent the work has been outside the main
stream of library automation, chiefly because the files
to be handled are small compared with even a British
provincial university library's total catalogue.
However, it is hoped that the results will be found
worth recording.   So far as Durham is concerned, the
end products in the form of quickly produced, variably
formatted, variously sorted, multi-copy catalogues
were well worth waiting for.

It is a pleasure to express our warmest appreciation
of the effort put in by Bob Oddy, who has worked long and
valiantly in bringing the project through all its stages
from the first enquiry to the fully documented operational
system we now have.

                              Agnes M. McAulay
                              University Librarian

July 1971

ACKNOWLEDGMENTS

I am chiefly indebted to Mr. Brian Cheesman
of Durham University Library, who specified what
was required of the automated system and possessed
unlimited patience in the face of all the snags
arising during development of the computer programs.
His careful study of this volume resulted in
numerous useful suggestions.

My thanks are also due to the members of the
Library staff who have been involved in the use
of the computer and have contributed much through
their comments and "experiences".   Particularly,
I should like to thank Mr. Jeremy Shearmur whose
comments and questions have influenced the contents
of this book and who supplied most of the material
for Appendix B.

The staff of the University of Durham Computer
Unit have given their advice on the technical side,
for which I am grateful.   I thank Mr. Brian Lander
for his help with the operational problems and his
advice during the writing of Chapter 2.

Mrs. Pat Croft has worked wonders with her
typewriter, and for her guidance on layout I am
most grateful.

R.N. Oddy
Computer Unit
University of Durham

CONTENTS

CONTENTS

To Evelyn

INTRODUCTION TO THE

LIBRARY FILE PROCESSING SYSTEM

The Library File Processing, or LFP, System is a tool for handling files of bibliographic records with the aid of an electronic digital computer. It encompasses the organization and structure of files both inside and outside the machine, the computer programs which create, maintain and operate upon files, the means of using the programs and the rules which the user must follow.

The LFP System has been devised at the request of Durham University Library to automate its Short Loan Collection of undergraduate reading material. Currently, the collection has some 2,500 titles and is reorganized termly to suit the courses given in the university.

Durham University owns, jointly with the University of Newcastle upon Tyne, an IBM 360 Model 67, known as NUMAC - the Northumbrian Universities Multiple Access Computer. The programs for the LFP System were written in IBM's PL/1 (Programming Language One) to run under the control of IBM System/360 Operating System (360/OS). On-line terminal facilities are not used by the present version of the LFP System, and communication with the computer is through 80-column punched cards and fast line printer.

The Records

The following textual or coded information can be recorded in the files for each item in the library:

(i)   Item number, an obligatory and unique record identification.

(ii) Type of publication (e.g. book, article, etc.).

(iii) Status (e.g. progress of order, temporary transfer from another collection, etc.).

(iv) Order details - agent, order and receipt dates, price, agent's report.

(v)   Courses for which the item is recommended.

(vi) Authors, titles, class numbers.

(vii) Publisher and date of publication.

A record need not contain information of every type. The significance of the information is largely irrelevant to the mechanical processes in the system; some of the fields mentioned can be used for other purposes at the discretion

of the library.   The author, title, class number and
publisher fields are of variable length, i.e. as long as the
number of characters written into them.   The remainder are
fixed length fields, in which information either conforms to
standard descriptions (e.g. prices or dates) or is codified
(e.g. agent's reports, courses).   Note that variable length
information must have control data to specify the beginning'
and end of the field.

The records are punched onto 80-column cards directly
from forms prepared in the Library.   The computer reads the
cards and stores the data on disks (these predominate over
magnetic tapes in NUMAC) from which files can subsequently
be read and processed.

The Programs

The file is the unit handled by the LFP System.   A
file may contain bibliographic or other types of data.
Stored in a "library" on a magnetic disk are programs which
perform simple operations upon files and have as their
result, or product, other files.   The more important operations of which the LFP System is capable are as follows:

(i)   Conversion of a file of bibliographic data from
      its form on punched cards to the internal form
      used on magnetic disks (or tapes).   The program
      does a certain amount of format checking, but it
      cannot spot errors of information content such
      as spelling mistakes and inconsistency among
      records in ways of writing the data.

(ii) Updating a file.   The contents of one file are
      used to modify the contents of another.   We can
      add records and remove them and can change
      records in any way.

(iii) Reproduction of files.   Files can be copied in
      their entirety or we can copy records selectively
      (i.e. extract a sub-file).

(iv) Sorting a file.   The records in a file are put
      into an alphabetical or numerical sequence (e.g.
      by item number, author, title or class number).

(v)   Merging files.   Two files, both previously
      sorted into one particular order, can be combined
      (merged) into a single file.

(vi) Printing files.   Files, or selected records from
      files, can be printed in a wide variety of formats.
      The user of the LFP System controls the format of
      a printout (to a fine degree) by means of direct-
      ives prepared on punched cards.

Note that the System contains no programs for accounting and is therefore not equipped to include a full ordering and accessions system, although the printing and file amendment aspects of the process can be done.   Nor has it been designed to handle a circulation system, since the particular collection for which it was intended requires only a simple single-access loan record.   However, the provision of a brief unique identification for each item means that an automated loan system could readily be run in conjunction.

Use of the Programs

LFP System programs should be regarded as building blocks for constructing more complex processes.   An operation which is complete from the library's point of view will normally consist of more than one of the processes mentioned above. For example, the production of an author catalogue at a time when the only file that is up to date is in item number order will require first a sort and then a printout.   Any number of basic processes can be combined to form a single composite one and the user expresses his requirements in a simple command language.   He writes, and then punches onto cards, a series of commands which invoke the programs one after the other and specify which files are to be involved in the task.

When the library has experience with the LFP System and has established its routine use of the system, certain standard card decks will be submitted to the computer with little preparation necessary and at regular intervals.   Within the limitations of the LFP System, the library will still retain the facilities for experimentation with its use of the computer. There is sufficient generality in the system for it to be useful to libraries other than the one for which it was written.   It is worth remarking that if two or more libraries use the same computer and file processing system, compatibility between their records will make projects such as the production of union catalogues relatively inexpensive extensions to the routine.

Modularity

The structure of the LFP System is modular.   That is to say that the programs comprising the system are mutually independent (though compatible) and any of them can be changed without affecting the others (by a programmer, maintaining certain file storage and other conventions).   It is also not difficult to incorporate new facilities.   The technical information which will be needed by anyone setting up a system of their own or adjusting the present one is contained in the manual The Library File Processing System Computer Programs (unpublished, available in the Computer Unit, University of Durham).

The Plan of this Book

The task of the book is to guide the reader in the use of the LFP System. The other guide to its use is experience in operating it - not every eventuality can be mentioned in a manual like this one. The user of the system needs knowledge of the following kinds:

(i)   How the files are organized. Chapter 3 is concerned with the organization of files of bibliographic data and describes the rules for preparing the data on punched cards. Details of the structure of files stored on disks are not necessary in the day to day running of the system.

(ii)   What the programs do. Chapters 4, 5 and 6 describe the functions of the important programs in the system. Chapter 8 deals with the automatic decoding of coded information, such as the course codes, and Chapter 9 describes the remaining non-central programs.

(iii)   How to use the programs. The reader is assumed to have no knowledge of computing and Chapter 2 introduces aspects relevant to the LFP System. We return to fill in details of the operation of the system in Chapter 7, after the major programs have been described. All the details given are in terms of the IBM System/360 Operating System (360/OS).

For successful operation of the LFP System, as with any library automation scheme, it is important to maintain contact with the computer staff. In the first place, the response from the computer must be reliable; deadlines have to be met and expert help may be required if unforeseen snags arise. Again, even with a small file (fewer than 10,000 items, say), the library's needs will be rather different from those of the average scientific worker, to whose requirements the computing service is usually geared.

2

This chapter is an attempt to ease the reader into an appreciation of the computing facility for which the Library File Processing System was written. The description will be largely specific to the LFP System. There exist brief, general introductions to computing written specially for the edification of librarians [1, 2, 3]. As has already been mentioned, the computer used is an IBM 360 Model 67 operated in a university environment. The LFP System runs under the control of the IBM System/360 Operating System (360/OS). It will be necessary to describe some of the more general aspects of the use of the computer and its operating system. The user of this system requires knowledge of the use of the computer's high capacity storage devices that the average scientific user does not need. On the other hand, he does not need programming ability.

2.1   *RESOURCES*

The cost of using the LFP System has not been calculated. In the university, individual departments are not charged for their use of the computer or related services, such as data preparation. There are, however, purely operational reasons for estimating in advance some of the resources which will be required. The operating system controls the devices involved in the input, output, storage and manipulation of data, and limits must be set on the demands of an individual computer job. Sometimes we specify an upper limit for a resource (processor time, for example) required by a task if we estimate that the operating system's assumption is not enough. If we underestimate in any respect, our job will be terminated prematuraly. Even when the operating system has accepted the job, the human operator has the final veto. He can cancel the execution if resources are requested which cannot be allocated to the job conveniently or efficiently at the time when the demand is made. The operator must be warned of special demands upon the computer system so that he can plan the session. The detailed rules which tell the computer user what is a normal job and how he should tell the operator and the computer of any abnormal requirements certainly vary from one installation to another and usually vary from time to time within one organization. In this chapter and in Chapter 7, some of the details must be regarded in this light.

Figure 2.1 is a schematic picture of the computer and its peripherals, as used by the LFP System. Let us examine briefly the various parts.

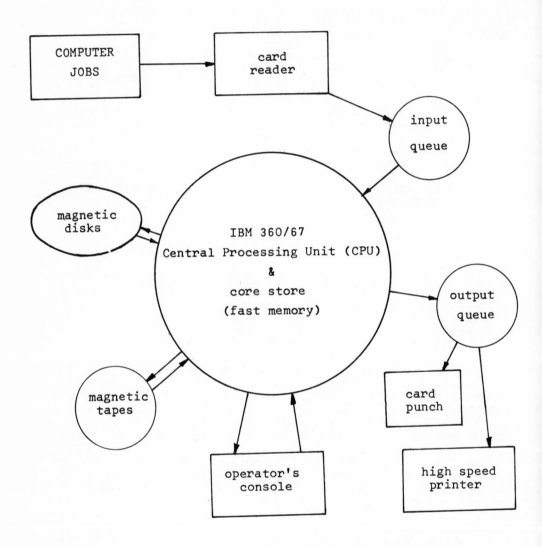

Figure 2.1   The Computing System

(i) The only way for the user of the LFP System to communicate his instructions to the computer is through the card reader. This means that in the first place, everything must be keypunched into 80-column cards. An explanation of what is meant by a "job" is given later (see section 2.2 of this chapter and, for LFP System specific details, see Chapter 7); for the moment, let it have a simple intuitive meaning - a task for the computer to do. A task, which is of arbitrary complexity, is specified by the user on punched cards and submitted to the operating staff. Throughout its progress in the system, the job is the unit handled by both the operators and the administrative functions of the computer.

(ii) The LFP System job is read and placed in a queue of jobs on a magnetic disk to await its turn for execution.

(iii) When the job reaches the head of the queue, the work is performed by the central processing unit. The core store is a memory device to which the CPU can refer very quickly indeed for individual characters or numbers. It is limited in size (e.g. less than 1%) in comparison to magnetic tapes and disks. Programs must be held in the core store while they are being executed, and it is thus shared by all computer users and cannot be used for long term storage.

(iv) High capacity storage (mass storage) is required by the LFP System for two main purposes; the storage of files (mainly of bibliographic records) and for holding the programs which comprise the system. The NUMAC installation has good magnetic disk storage facilities but only two magnetic tape drives and jobs which use disks are "preferred" to those using tapes. Information is recorded magnetically on concentric tracks on the surface of a disk; several disks are set one above the other on a single spindle and the whole is called a disk volume. Connected to the computer are several disk drives upon which the disk volumes can be mounted as required. NUMAC has the IBM 2314 disk storage facility. While they are mounted, the disks spin at a rate of about 2400 revolutions per minute, so it does not take very long to locate and read blocks of information from the tracks into the core store and, conversely, to write data from the core store to a disk. The capacity of a disk volume depends to a large extent upon the way in which the information is organized. About 180,000 of Durham University

Library's relatively short records would fit into
one volume. In fact, at the time of writing, the
two short loan collections together have a stock
of about 3500 items, so we are using about 2% of
a 2314 disk volume for the main files of bibliographic records. Another 2% is used for all the
programs in the LFP System. The files, like the
programs, are stored on a public disk because they
are not yet large enough to warrant the purchase
of a private one, and because operator action is
then at a minimum.

(v) The usual form of output is printed output. It
is also possible to have cards punched by the
computer. Both the line-printer and the card
punch are relatively slow devices and the output
reaches them indirectly, via a queue on a disk.
In this way jobs with a lot of output do not hold
up other jobs while they use the printer or punch
and, on the other hand, those devices are not
idle while jobs with little output are being
executed.

(vi) There is a typewriter console close to the computer
which is the means of communication between the
operator and the computer. For many jobs in a
university, the operator need do nothing, except
to put the cards into the reader and to associate
printout with cards afterwards, and the LFP System
jobs will often require no more attention than
that. Jobs usually progress through the computing
system without operator intervention but if
anything unusual is required, the user must
specify that the job be held in the input queue
until the operator releases it, when convenient,
by typing a message on his console. Such jobs
are called hold jobs.

Figure 2.2 contains estimates of the computer resource
requirements for processing files of different sizes. The
first column gives the size of the file. It should be
emphasized that the larger of the two files maintained at
Durham University has not, so far, contained more than 2500
book records. The table, therefore, consists mostly of
theoretical estimates. The second column in figure 2.2 is
the estimated storage requirement for the file. A permanent
allocation of storage space will be required for the main
file, as given in the table, and for a "back-up" copy (which
is needed for the sake of safety). Arrangements will usually
have to be made with the computer service department for space
on public disk volumes and there could be difficulty if the
file occupies more than 10% of a volume. Magnetic tapes and
private disks can be used and the library can profit especially
from the latter if it has a large file or several smaller ones
to maintain.

Number of book records*	Storage % of volume**	CPU time given in minutes,seconds				Working Storage for Sorting % of volume**
		Copying	Updating	Printing	Sorting	
2,500	1.4	0:04	0:13	0:17	2:20	3.5
5,000	2.8	0:07	0:26	0:35	5:00	7
10,000	5.6	0:15	0:50	1:10	10:50	14
20,000	11.2	0:30	1:40	2:10	23:30	28
40,000	22.5	1:00	3:20	4:30	48:30	56
60,000	34	1:30	5:00	6:40	72:00	85

* The size of the records is assumed to be as for those of Durham University Library, i.e. on average 98 characters of textual information.

** Storage is expressed as a percentage of a 2314 disk volume, upon which there are 4000 tracks.

Figure 2.2   Table of requirements according to file size

Four important file processes are mentioned, with estimates of the central processing unit time demanded.   All the LFP System procedures are what is called "input/output bound", i.e. their speed of execution depends predominantly upon the rate at which information can be transferred between the core store and mass storage.   As is explained in a later section on the Operating System, several things can be happening in the machine at once and the computer can usually be getting on with something else while our job is waiting for a record to be read from a disk. The CPU time is the time for which our program has the processor. The elapse time is reckoned from when the program starts to when it terminates and that can be 3 or 4 times the CPU time.   The elapse time is impossible to estimate reliably in advance because it depends on what else is going on in the computer.   For jobs of less than about 8 minutes CPU time, the elapse time need not worry us.   It can be seen from the table in figure 2.2 that the

CPU times for copying, updating and printing files of up to 60,000 records are estimated to be quite short, whereas the process of sorting a large file is extremely long.   If a file of more than about 10,000 records is to be sorted, the advice of the operational staff should be sought.   They should also be able to advise on how the large quantity of disk working storage (last column of the table) which the sorting process requires might be allocated during the job.

A printing job will usually not require a lot of CPU time, but it may occupy the printer for a long time and the computer staff should be consulted if more than 10,000 lines are to be printed by one job.   They will also be able to advise on the use of special printer stationery, for printing more than one copy using carbon paper for example.

Some of the programs can be used to punch cards but one is discouraged from large scale usage of the computer's card punch because it is rather a slow device.

The user of the computer will minimize delays in processing by arranging that as many as possible of his jobs are short and require no special action by the operator.   The LFP System was designed to be flexible and easy to operate for small files, and is less suitable for files larger than 10,000 items because there are then other problems which it does not attempt to solve.   Figure 2.3 summarizes typical operational rules for submitting a job to a system such as the IBM 360/OS.

Type of Job	CPU Time	Lines Printed	Cards Punched	Other
Normal	<10 mins.	<3,000	<200	Frequently mounted public disk volumes only
Hold	10-20 mins.	3,000-10,000	200-1,000	Other disk volumes and magnetic tapes
by special arrangement	>20 mins.	>10,000	>1,000	>2 disks simultaneously. Special printer stationery

Figure 2.3   Guide to Operational requirements. Put mental ticks in the boxes according to the demands of the job;   the tick nearest the bottom of the table determines the job type.

2.2   *THE OPERATING SYSTEM* (360/*OS*)

We shall not discuss the operating system in great depth.
The reader who needs or is interested in the details should
consult IBM's introductory manuals [4, 5].   At the beginning
of a daily computer session, the control program or supervisor
is copied into the core store (from a disk) and given control.
Typically, a control program might take up 10% of the
available core storage.   The supervisor has responsibility
for loading programs into other parts of the core store from
program libraries, passing control to them to do the work
which we have requested, managing all the input and output
devices (including mass storage) and recovering from the
catastrophic situations which can arise out of our (and others')
errors.

The operating system recognizes three kinds of object:

(i)   Programs, which it loads into core storage.

(ii)   Resources, such as core storage, files and processor
time, which it allocates to satisfy the needs of the
programs.

(iii)   Job control statements, which specify the programs
and resources required by the user and are expressed
in the Job Control Language (JCL).

A Job is an independent piece of work or task for the
computer to perform.   It is composed of one or more job steps.
Each job step requests the execution of a program and the
steps are performed one after the other in the order specified
in the job.   We extend the meaning of job so that the actual
deck of punched cards upon which the task is specified is also
referred to as the job.

The core store is divided into several partitions and
each can contain a program.   The supervisor shares the processor
time between the programs.   This is called Multiprogramming -
the computer is effectively doing several tasks at once.   When
a job reaches the head of the input queue, it is allocated a
partition of core storage and all the steps in the job are done
within the same partition.   There is usually a variety of
partition sizes and the job must specify which size it requires
so that the supervisor does not put it into one that is too
small.

Programs are written by computer users in a number of
Programming Languages.   Each language has a compiler, which
is itself a program and is a part of the operating system.
The compiler reads a program in the source language and translates
it into the machine's own language;   the user's program is being
treated as data by the compiler.   The program produced by the

compiler is usually not complete because it calls upon other programs to do standard operations. These, previously written, programs will be stored in "libraries" on disk and there is an important program in the operating system called the Linkage Editor which gathers together and organizes all the parts to form a program which is ready to be executed. A typical job for 360/OS consists of three job steps. The first program to be executed is a compiler, then the linkage editor finishes the preparation of the user's program and the final step is the execution of that program.

LFP System jobs are slightly different in that an extra step is performed at the beginning. The user specifies his requirements in a simple command language and the first step of the job converts his commands into a PL/1 program which is then processed in the normal, three step manner.

2.3 THE LIBRARY FILE PROCESSING SYSTEM

The central part of the LFP System is a library of programs on a disk volume. There are programs which create, maintain, sort and print files of bibliographic data, and do related tasks and there are other programs which are used by them. These programs have been written in PL/1 and they are already compiled. To use them, we write a simple program of commands, each of which invokes a program in the library. We can thus have any combination of tasks performed and involve any file in the process.

The other important part specifically written for the LFP System is a program called the Library File Program Generator, which reads a program of commands and generates firstly a PL/1 program to call upon the appropriate task programs and secondly some instructions for the linkage editor so that the programs can be assembled in such a way as to economize on the core storage required by the final program.

The remaining important programs used by the LFP System are the PL/1(F) Compiler and the Linkage Editor; both are parts of the IBM System/360 Operating System.

Files are created by the programs in formats which are peculiar to the LFP System. The operating system finds space on the disks for the files and keeps them or deletes them as requested by the user in the job control statements. Records are constructed, processed and examined by the programs in the LFP System library. Space on disk volumes is allocated in organizational units called data-sets, and in the LFP System one data-set holds one file. When the operating system creates a data-set on a disk, it must be told the initial size required (data-sets can expand as necessary after their creation). The user must give a unique name to each data-set which he keeps on a disk volume and he is responsible for cataloguing his data-sets, that is he must keep a record of what data-sets he has and what files they contain.

A summary of a normal LFP System job follows. The asterisks mark those parts which the user must supply.

* (i)   A program of commands. Each command specifies a process and the files to be involved in it.

  (ii) The program is converted to a PL/1 program by the library file program generator.

 (iii) The new PL/1 program is translated by the PL/1(F) Compiler.

  (iv) Program and library components are combined by the Linkage Editor.

*   (v) The final program is executed. The files mentioned in the commands must be defined for the operating system by associating them with data-sets or devices.

* (vi) Various types of data cards to be read by the program.

We have used the term program in quite a wide ranging sense. There are programs written by the LFP System user in the command language, programs to translate them into equivalent programs (in another language) which call yet other programs which do the required work and all this operates under the supervision of the 360/OS control program. Operating systems are designed in modular fashion and the LFP System follows suit. This means that they are composed of independent pieces of programming and if we make distinctions between programs and subroutines or subprograms, we shall find it difficult to know where to draw the line. So we call them all programs.

Most of the remaining chapters contain descriptions of LFP System programs which can be invoked by commands. Some remarks are necessary at this point concerning the organization of the descriptions. Each program (or command) description contains information under the headings Command, Function and Notes, Data Definition Cards, Computer Time and Completion Codes. We shall discuss each of these in turn.

1. Command

A prototype command is given and followed by an explanation of each part of the command. The user should model his command upon the prototype, copying the uppercase characters and the terminating semicolon exactly and substituting his own, appropriate, text for the symbolic names which are underlined in the prototype. The second word in the prototype command is the name of the program being invoked and the words to the right of it are called parameters. Some of the parameters represent names, for example file names, and these must obey the following rules.

(i)   A name consists of from 1 to 7 characters.

(ii) The first character must be a letter, others may be letters or digits.

(iii) There must be no spaces within a name.

Example

The prototype command for the sorting function is

label SORT infile sortfile sequence ;

"label", "infile", "sortfile" and "sequence" are all symbolic names, and an actual command in a user's program might be

A SORT LBK LAU SEQ601 ;

A detailed account of the use of the command language is given in Chapter 7.

2.   Function and Notes

Paragraphs under this heading describe the purpose of the command and the roles played by the files involved.

3.   Data Definition Cards

A data definition card is a particular type of job control card (see Section 2.4 and Chapter 7). Under this heading appears a list of the files which need data definition cards and any information which is peculiar to the relevant command. The general rule is that each file referred to (including implicit references) in the program must be defined just once on data definition cards in the job.

4.   Computer Time

A formula for calculating processor time (CPU time), based on the amount of data and estimated from experience at Durham, is given. This should be used to estimate the CPU time requirement for the final job step (the operating system will terminate the step after one minute of CPU time unless we have asked for more).

5.   Completion Codes

The computer finishes each task with a code to
indicate its outcome.   The codes most frequently used
are:

(i)   0.   Normal execution.

(ii)   4.   The user is warned that certain situations
were encountered.   The execution may have
been unsuccessful.

(iii)   8.   An error was detected.   The task will not
have been completed.

(iv)   12.   As for 8, but more serious.

If the command has been given a label, i.e. a reference
name, the completion code can be used to determine whether
other commands in the same program are obeyed.

2.4   *JOB CONTROL LANGUAGE (JCL)*

This section explains the user's means of communication
with the operating system.   There is little detail at this
stage.   Most of the information required by the LFP System
user is contained in Chapter 7.   A job for the computer is
a sequence of program executions.   The user specifies his
requirements by constructing a deck of cards containing
job control statements and, usually, some data for the
programs.   The cards are organized in groups as follows:

Job information
job step 1 information
job step 2 information
.   .   .
end-of-job card

Cards containing job control statements always have the
character / punched in both the 1st and 2nd columns.

Job Information

The first card of a job must always be the JOB card.
It signifies the start of the job, identifies the originator,
specifies upper limits for printed and punched output if more
is required than the assumed limits and tells the scheduler
part of the control program which size of core storage partition is required.   If the job is a hold job (see figure 2.3),
a HOLD card should follow the JOB card.   The HOLD card is
not, strictly speaking, a job control statement.   It should
contain a brief message to the operator to tell him what
resources are required by the job and its effect is to inhibit
the automatic scheduling of the job so that the operator can
release it for execution at his convenience.

Job Step Information

At the beginning of each step is an EXEC statement, which
names the program which is to be placed into the partition of
core store and given control.   (This program may call upon
others.)   The EXEC statement is followed by Data Definition
(DD) statements which link the files used by the program with
devices.   If a data-set is a deck of 80-column punched cards,
then those cards should be included in the job step with a
special DD statement heading them.   Figure 2.4 is a diagram
which may make the process clear.   Suppose that a program
called PROGA has been written to read its data from two files
called INFILE1 and INFILE2 and to write (or print) information
into a file called OUTFILE.   The EXEC card brings PROGA from
a program library into the user's partition.   We now have
inside the large box in the diagram the program and its internal
input and output channels with metaphorical plugs on the ends.
Outside the box are the physical devices, with the data-sets
on them, and DD cards which determine what devices are plugged
into the program's channels of communication.

There are a few other types of information which can be
given in the EXEC statement.   The only one which we mention
now is processor time.   The operating system will normally
allow a job step no more than 1 minute of CPU time and that
is ample for the first three steps of a LFP System job.   We
can increase the allowance for a step by using the TIME
parameter in the EXEC statement.   If the time required to
complete a step exceeds the allowance, the step and the whole
job are terminated.

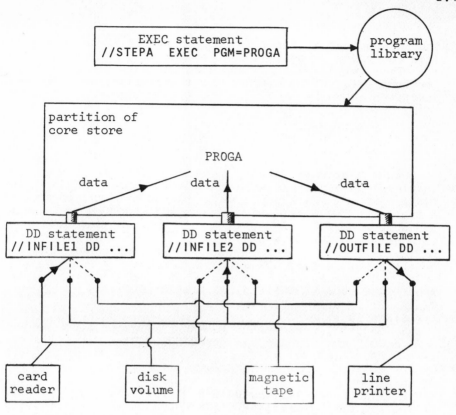

Figure 2.4   A job step

Catalogued Procedures

The task of constructing a job can be made easier and
less error-prone by the facility for retrieving sets of job
control statements stored in a special library on a disk
volume.   A catalogued procedure is such a set of statements
defining or partially defining a sequence of job steps.
The steps may be incomplete and in fact that is often necessary
because some of the information can only be supplied when an
actual job is run.   A catalogued procedure is invoked by a
special form of EXEC statement.   One must imagine that this
EXEC statement is replaced by the statements stored in the
catalogued procedure.   Information in the catalogued procedure
is supplemented or overridden by DD statements in the submitted
job.

The LFP System is best operated with the aid of a
catalogued procedure and the one in use in Durham University
is set out in Appendix C.   All that the user supplies are

the definitions of the file containing the commands for the first step and of the files which the fourth step processes. The other two steps (PL/1 compilation and linkage editing) are complete, so the user need not explicitly mention them in the job.

2.5   A SAMPLE JOB

This section is simply a preview with little explanation. Chapter 7 is concerned with the details of assembling LFP System jobs.   The example below represents what might actually be keypunched onto cards and submitted as a complete job to sort a file of bibliographic records (file LBK in data-set DUL01LBK on a disk volume) into author order (file LAU) and then print the sorted file in the format specified on the cards in file CONTROL.

```
//DUL01ABC  JOB  (0001,L23,,3),LIBRARY,CLASS=C
//S1    EXEC  DLFPMCLG,TIME.G=(5,0)
//M.SYSIN DD *
   CAT  PROGRAM;  /*COMMANDS TO MAKE AUTHOR CATALOGUE*/
        SORT LBK LAU SEQ601;  /*AUTHOR SORT*/
        PRINT CONTROL 72;
        END;
/*
//G.WORK2   DD   UNIT=2314,VOL=SER=UNE020,SPACE=(TRK,(40,5))
//G.WORK3   DD   UNIT=2314,VOL=SER=UNE030,SPACE=(TRK,(40,5))
//G.WORK4   DD   UNIT=2314,VOL=SER=UNE040,SPACE=(TRK,(40,5))
//G.LBK  DD  DSN=DUL01LBK,UNIT=2314,VOL=SER=UNE040,DISP=SHR
//G.LAU  DD  UNIT=2314,VOL=SER=UNE999,SPACE=(TRK,(60,5))
//G.CONTROL  DD  *
     LIST FILE LAU;
     /*THESE INSTRUCTIONS CONTROL THE LAYOUT
          OF THE CATALOGUE*/
     SELECT ITEMS IF '#300=BDEF';
     SPACE 1;
     2, (#102,3,#601), CONT IN 8, STOP IN 95;
     +4, TAB 25, #701, CONT IN 27, STOP IN 95;
     END;
/*
//
```

When the library has established its routine use of the system, it will naturally have a collection of commonly used jobs ready for submitting to the computer.

REFERENCES

1   COX, N.S.M., J.D. DEWS and J.L. DOLBY
    The Computer and the Library
    University of Newcastle upon Tyne Library.   1966.
    Chapter III.   Computers: their Uses and Limitations.
    pp.27-43

2   DEWS, J. DAVID
    Computers and Libraries
    Program No. 6, July 1967.   pp.25-33

3   KIMBER, RICHARD T.
    Automation in Libraries
    Pergamon Press.   1968.
    Chapter 2.   Introduction to Computers.   By ANNE H. BOYD.
    pp.18-34

4   IBM System/360 Operating System: Introduction, Form C28-6534.
    IBM Corp., Data Processing Division, White Plains, N.Y.

5   IBM System/360 Operating System: Concepts and Facilities,
    Form C28-6535.
    IBM Corp., Data Processing Division, White Plains, N.Y.

In this chapter, we do some of the groundwork on files
with specific reference to the Library File Processing System.
Firstly, some basic words are defined and the structure of
files is described in general terms.   Then the forms in which
the files are stored and the methods employed by the computer
programs to process them are discussed, again in quite general
terms.   Finally we get down to details of the preparation of
files for the computer.

3.1   *FILE STRUCTURE*

File.   We define a File as a collection of records in some
    sequence.   The records can be in some sort of numerical
    or alphabetic order or just in the order they were
    thought of.   The order is mentioned simply to emphasize
    the sequential nature of the file processing done by
    this system.

Record.   The Record is the conceptual unit of information in
    the file.   When we are thinking of the file as a file
    of bibliographic information, the record is the aggregate
    of information pertaining to one book (or to whatever
    the bibliographic unit is).

Item.   An Item is a record in this particular context.   That
    is, an item is a bibliographic record.   Thus, when the
    word record is used, we will usually be thinking about the
    file from some other point of view.   For example, if the
    file is punched into 80-column cards, we might use the
    word record to mean all the characters on one card, even
    though an item spans several cards.

Element.   The item can contain several different types of
    information.   For example, most items will contain the
    name of an author and a title.   These sub-units within
    an item are called Elements (or sometimes Fields, although
    that word is used slightly differently in connection with
    the printing of lists).   In this system, there is a limit
    to the number of elements an item may have and there are
    certain size restrictions, which vary from element to
    element.   The semantic significance of the different
    elements is largely at the discretion of the user of the
    system.   An item need not contain an element from every
    possible category.

Tag.   The elements within an item must be identified.   There
    are two methods.   The first is to identify it by its
    position in the record as, for example, on a catalogue
    card.   The other method is to attach a label to each

element saying what sort of information it is.   These
labels are called Tags or Element Identifiers.   The LFP
System uses both methods at various times.   When tags
are used, they are numeric.

3.2   *FILE REPRESENTATION AND STORAGE*

Before files of bibliographic data can exist within the
computer they must pass through two intermediate forms in the
LFP System. The first of these is a bundle of slips of paper
written by a librarian.   The other is a deck of 80-column
cards key-punched by the data preparation service directly
from the slips.   These, of course, are readable by the computer
and are normally reformatted for reasons of efficiency before
being stored on a magnetic recording medium such as a disk or
a tape.

General comments will be made at this stage about the
different forms of file.   Details of the first and second
representations are given later in this chapter.

Files on Paper Forms

Forms are printed with blank areas for all the elements
which might be required in the items.   Clearly, it is convenient
if one form contains one item, but it would have to be a very
large form indeed to allow for every possibility.   One can
design quite a small form which is of adequate capacity for the
large majority of items and which can also be used as a continuation form for the remaining large or awkward items.   The forms
used by Durham University Library have the numeric element tags
printed on them for the benefit of the card punch operators as
well as an element name (e.g. "author") for the use of the
librarian who fills them in.

Items on Punched Cards - External Files

Items are punched directly from the forms prepared in the
library.   Each element is typed with the appropriate tag
preceding it and a special terminating character following it.
Another special character is used to separate the items in a
file.   The format is fairly free, that is items and elements
can be arranged without regard to the exact position on the
cards.   We shall refer to a file of items organized in this
way as an External File, or File in External Format, because
it is in the form that is used outside the machine.

Files in Internal Format

External files are not organized for efficient processing
they are just readable.   In the Internal Format, elements are
identified by their position in the item.   The format is
described in Appendix A; it is slightly complicated to allow -
without too much wastage - for the variability of some of the

field lengths and of the number of fields included in an item.
Internal files are created and manipulated by the computer
programs. They can be stored on disks, magnetic tapes or
other high capacity storage devices, but not on punched cards
unless they are first converted to the external format. In
Durham University, the internal files are kept on disks.

Note on Card Files

A Card File is a file in which the information is divided
into records of 80 characters, regardless of the nature of the
information. Both of the following are card files:

A deck of punched 80-column cards
A file of 80-character records (Card Images) on a disk

Programs which read or punch real cards will also read
or write card files on disk or magnetic tape. External files
are card files (although not necessarily vice-versa) and can
exist on disks and be read by programs from there. We use
other card files in this system and they are described in later
chapters.

3.3   COMPUTER HANDLING OF FILES

Firstly, all files are given names, which are chosen by
the user.

Secondly, the bibliographic files are always handled
Sequentially in the LFP System. That is to say that a file
is a sequence of records and the programs which read them will
"see" the records in the order in which they were written.
Selection of items with certain characteristics from a file
is done by reading the file from start to finish, testing each
item and selecting or rejecting it on the result of the test.
Sorting is the process of rearranging a file into some
predefined sequence which may be different from the existing
one.

We now discuss briefly the two basic file operations used
by all the programs - reading files and writing files.

Input

This is the straightforward process of a program reading
a file sequentially, starting at the first record. Note that
if a deck of punched cards is specified as an input file, the
program can read it only once during a job.

Output

The program writes, punches or prints a file. If the
file is written onto a disk, there are several possibilities.

(i)   The file is <u>New</u>.   That is, the name of the file does not refer to any existing file.   At the end of the process, we have the file of records as written by the program.

(ii) The file is <u>Extant</u>.   That is, the name of the file refers to a file previously written.   In this case, there are two possibilities.   Usually we replace, or <u>overwrite</u>, the whole file by another one and the result is the same as if the file had been a new one.   It is also possible to add the new records on at the end of the old file.

Many processes require <u>work</u> files.   These hold sequences of records which are needed at certain stages in a job but are not required to be saved at the end.   Typically, the following simple processes might be performed upon a work file during one job.

1.   Create the new work file called WORK1, for example.

2.   Write WORK1, i.e. write a sequence of records into WORK1.

3.   Read WORK1.

4.   Overwrite WORK1, i.e. replace the extant file by a new sequence of records.

5.   Read WORK1.   This time we get the file as written in step 4.

Updating Files

The updating process is introduced at this point because of its implication for the format of internal files.   Only files in internal format can participate in updating.

Updating in the LFP System can be summarized as follows. The contents of one internal file (called the <u>Main file</u>), modified by the contents of another internal file (called the <u>Updating file</u>), form a third internal file (called the <u>New Main file</u>).   Because the updating is done sequentially, both the main file and the updating file must be in the same sequence (by item number).   The new main file will also be in that sequence.   The updating takes place item by item and there are three possible actions.

1.   An item from the updating file is added to the main file.

2.   An item in the main file is amended by one in the updating file.

3.   An item is removed from the main file.

60-character set	48-character set		Collating Sequence (in Sorts etc.)
blank	blank		LOW
.	.		
<			
(	(		
+	+		
|			
&			
£	£	special significance in external format files	
*	*		
)	)		
;			
¬		"not"	
-	-	"minus" or hyphen	
/	/		
,	,	comma	
%			
_		underscore	
>			
?			
:			
#		"number" has special significance throughout	
@			
'	'	single apostrophe or "quote"	
=	=		
A to Z	A to Z	upper case letters	
0 to 9	0 to 9	numerals (0 means "zero")	HIGH

Figure 3.1   Character Sets

We are concerned here with the second activity, amending items. This is done by replacing elements as desired and leaving the remaining elements untouched. The amending item in the updating file will contain only those elements which are replacements; the others will simply be absent. There is then the problem of signifying in the amending item the removal of an element from the item in the main file. The solution is to distinguish between null elements and irrelevant (and therefore absent) elements, and an internal file in which this distinction is made is in <u>Updating Format</u>. Otherwise, it is in <u>Normal Format</u>.

The process of converting a file from external to internal format produces a file in updating format. The updating format is only significant when the file acts as an updating file. The new main file is always in normal format.

3.4 CONSTRUCTING ITEMS FOR COMPUTER FILES

We now describe the practical details of preparing data in the external file format. Firstly, in figure 3.1 are listed the characters available on the NUMAC printers and card punch keyboards. Printing at Durham has been limited to the 48-character set. The types of elements which it is possible to include in an item are in the table of figure 3.2

There follows a list of rules and notes for the various types of elements.

(i) Element #100 must be present in every item.

(ii) The characters #, £ and * have special significance and may not be included in any element.

(iii) One-character codes (elements #102, #203, #300, #301) should be characters chosen from a predefined code list. The code list may contain any character.

(iv) The three-character codes (elements #200 and #401 to #499) are alphabetic.

(v) The date elements (#201 and #202) can be written in various forms in the external files and are converted to a standard form for the internal files. The date 9th November 1969 can be represented by either

9/11/69
or **091169**

In the first form, spacing is not significant but spaces should not occur between the digits of a number. There must be three numbers: day, month and year.

The second form must consist of 6 digits without embedded spaces; two for the day, two for the month and two for the year.

26

Element Tag	Field Size in Characters	Element Name	Comments (See also Appendix B)
#100	5	item number	This is the only obligatory element in an item
#101	5	replacement item number	Used only in an updating file to change an item number
#102	1	type code	Indicates the type of document, e.g. book, journal
#200	3	agent code	
#201	-	order date	) The format of these
#202	-	date received	) is restricted
#203	1	agent report code	
#300	1	status code	Indicates the state of an order and the availability of the item
#301	1	(unused)	
#302	-	price	Format restricted
#401-#499	3	course code(s)	Indicates for which courses the item is provided
#500	≤50	date of publication	) i. There is a) restriction on) the total field
#601-#699	≤2413	author(s)	) size of these) elements)
#701-#799	≤2413	title(s)	) ii. By "author",) "title", "class) number" we really
#801-#899	≤2413	class number(s)	) mean heading for) filing in author,) title or class
#900	≤2413	publisher	) number sequence

Figure 3.2   Table of Element Types

27

(vi)   The price element (#302) can be written in several forms and is again converted to a standard form for internal files. The "£ s. d." price £2.10.6 can be written either

2.10.6

or **021006**

There must be 3 numbers in the first form: pounds, shillings and pence.

In the other form, there must be 6 digits; two for pounds, two for shillings and two for pence.

The decimal price £2.50 should be written in one of the following forms

D2.50

or **2.50**

in which cases there must be two numbers, one for pounds and one for pennies

or **D00250**

that is the letter D followed by 5 digits, three for the pounds and two for the pennies.

Note that prices less than £1 must be written in one of the above forms. For example, 45p could be represented by

0.45

or **D0.45**

or **D00045**

or **0.9.0**

(vii)   The variable length fields (#500,#601-#699,#701-#799, #801-#899,#900) can contain any characters except #, £ and *, and can be of any length up to the maximum values given in figure 3.2 under the constraint that the total size of the item is limited as indicated in note (x) below.

(viii)   Additional Headings

Ranges of element tags are available so that additional elements can be provided for items which should be filed in more than one place in certain sequences, i.e. which might have added entries in conventional library catalogues. The four ranges are #401 to #499 (courses), #601 to #699 (authors), #701 to #799 (titles) and #801 to #899 (class numbers). In preparing new items or amendments to items, additional elements can be included by using the next available tag in the appropriate range. Any individual element with a tag in these ranges can be updated.

Note that there are no elements with the tags #400, #600, #700 or #800.

(ix) No two elements in one item may have the same tag.

(x) There is a limit to the size of an item in an internal file, and this restricts the total combined length of the variable fields Author, Title, Class number and Publisher to just under 2400 characters, or about twenty times the normal. In precise terms the sum of all the characters in fields 401 to 900, plus 4 times the number of authors, titles and class numbers, may not exceed 2417, or

$$L_c + L_d + L_p + \sum_e (L_e + 4) \leq 2417$$

where L_c = sum of lengths of course elements (3, 6, 9 characters etc.)

L_d = length of date of publication

L_p = length of publisher

$\sum_e (L_e + 4)$ = sum of lengths of author(s), title(s), class number(s) with 4 added to each.

Punching Items on Cards

We now give the rules for transferring information to the 80-column cards in external format.

(i) An element is punched as follows.

<u>tag</u> <u>text</u> £

<u>tag</u> is one of the element tags given in figure 3.2. It is punched as the # character followed by an appropriate 3-digit number. Spaces are allowed between the # and the number, but not embedded in the number.

<u>text</u> is the actual element. When the item is converted to internal format, any spaces at the beginning and end of the <u>text</u> will be removed. Then the element will be entered unchanged into the internally formatted item (unless it is one of the elements #201, #202 or #302 – see notes (v) and (vi) above).

£ acts as a terminating character.

Example: The following are all equivalent to a primary author field of "SMITH H." in an internal file

```
#601 SMITH H.£
#601SMITH H.£
#   601    SMITH H.    £
```

(ii)   The elements of an item are punched one after another
       in any order whatever and, optionally, with spaces
       between them.   The last element in an item must be
       followed by a * (spaces may intervene).   The * acts
       as an end-of-item character.

(iii) If an item contains, in the syntactic place of a punched
       element, either

                        DELETE
                  or DELETE £

       then that item is intended to cause the deletion from
       a file of the item with the specified element #100,
       or item number.   All other elements in the punched
       item are superfluous.   A "delete" item is only
       meaningful in a file which is destined to be an
       updating file.

       Example: Any of the following items could be used to
       specify the deletion of item number "D2371".

           #100 D2371£ DELETE £ *
           #100 D2371 £ DELETE *
           DELETE #100 D2371 £ *
           DELETE #100 D2371£ #601 JEANS J.£ *

       In the last item, the author element is included simply
       to remind us which item is being deleted; it is not
       used to identify the item by the computer.

(iv)   In the simplest case, when punching a file in external
       format, we ignore the card boundaries and imagine that
       the cards are stuck together in a long strip.   If the
       end of a card comes in the middle of a word, we just
       carry on in column 1 of the next card.   There are
       occasions when it is useful (or wise!) to have the
       cards numbered and in that case the numbers are punched
       in the last few columns of the cards.   When laying
       out the elements and items, the card columns containing
       the numbers are ignored; we imagine that we have, for
       example, 72-column cards instead of 80-column cards.

   Appendix B shows how items might be punched.   The appendix
also contains copies of the instructions as used in Durham
University by library staff writing the forms and by card punch
operators transferring the data to cards.

Some of the LFP programs can now be described and we start with three important functions:

(i) Conversion of bibliographic files from external format to internal format, which is the tool for getting files into the machine.

(ii) Updating files in internal format.

(iii) Copying internal files either in their entirety or selectively.

The descriptions include prototype commands to invoke the programs written in the form described in Chapter 2.

4.1 *FILE CONVERSION (EXTERNAL TO INTERNAL FORMAT)*

1. Command

<u>label</u> **FINPUT** <u>extfile</u> <u>column</u> <u>switch</u> <u>intfile</u> <u>code102</u>
<u>code203</u> <u>code300</u> <u>code301</u> ;

<u>label</u> is optional and is any name by which the command can be referred.

FINPUT is the name of the file input program, which converts the items in external format in the card file called <u>extfile</u> into a file of items in internal format called <u>intfile</u>.

<u>extfile</u> is an input card file name representing an external file.

<u>column</u> is a number not exceeding 80. It specifies the last column from which data is to be taken (e.g. 80 if the whole card is read, 72 if columns 73-80 are ignored as in the case of numbered cards).

<u>switch</u> is replaced, in practice, by either ON if a printed copy of the card file is required, or OFF if the printout is to be suppressed. If the switch is OFF, cards with errors are the only ones printed.

<u>intfile</u> is the name of the output internal file. It can be new or extant (see section 3.3).

<u>code102</u> is a string of the characters which are admissible codes for element #102.

31

code203 is a string of the characters which are admissible codes for element #203.

code300 is a string of the characters which are admissible codes for element #300.

code301 is a string of the characters which are admissible codes for element #301.

The last four parameters are used for checking purposes.

2.   Function and Notes

FINPUT reads the external file extfile item by item, performing certain checks and writing the valid items to intfile in the internal Updating format (see section 3.3).

The checks performed are as follows:

(i)   Format checks, so that it is quite clear what comprises each element and item.

(ii) Element checks.   Some of the elements are restricted in the form that they can take.   For example, the item number (#100) must be 5 characters long and dates and prices must make sense.   The codes entered in elements #102, #203, #300 and #301 can be checked against the lists which form the last four parameters of the command.

There are two special cases.   If the parameter is an empty string,

$$'',$$

that is to say a string of zero characters, no checking is done on the corresponding coded element.   If the parameter is a space,

$$'\ ',$$

then no code will be acceptable for that element, so every item with that element present will be rejected.

In the event of errors shown up by format or element checks, the remainder of the item is ignored and no corresponding item will be written to intfile.   Messages are printed to describe the nature of the error.

The two files involved are of different types, one is a card file and the other is an internal file.   The two file names in the FINPUT command must therefore be different.

3.   Data Definition Cards

Job control cards are required to define the data-sets associated with extfile and intfile.

(i)   extfile will be a card file, usually on punched cards submitted with the job; or it may be a previously created file on a disk or magnetic tape.

(ii) Space requirements of an internally formatted file

intfile is an output file which is either new or extant.   If it is new, a new data-set must be created for it, which must be provided with enough space for the internal file.   The space is difficult to esti-mate accurately in advance.   It depends on how elements numbered from #401 onwards are used.   The table below can be used as a rough guide, so long as the average number of #401-#499 elements (C) and the average total size of variable length elements per item (L) is known.

Table of number of items per track on a 2314 disk

L \\ C	0	40	80	120	160	200	300	400
0	100	60	38	28	23	19	12.5	10
5	75	50	33	27	21.5	18	12.5	10
10	60	43	30	25	20	17.5	12.5	10
20	50	37.5	27	21.5	19	16	11.5	9.5

This table is neither complete nor perfectly reliable (it was produced by a computer simulation).   If the figure obtained from the table is i items per track, and the number of items in the file is n, then let

t = nearest whole number below n/i, and let

s = nearest whole number below $\dfrac{n}{101}$

If either t or s is zero, increase it to 1.

Request space as follows: SPACE=(TRK,(t,s))

Example

In the file for the Short Loan Collection in Durham
University's Main Library, the average number of
course codes per item is 1.13, and there are, on
average, 64.1 characters of variable length information per item.

Looking at the table, the value of i is 45, roughly.

Suppose we are creating a file of 250 typical new
items,

then n=250, t=5, s=1

so we require SPACE=(TRK,(5,1))

4.   Computer Time

Central processor times for FINPUT vary between 5 and 10
seconds per 100 items, depending on the size of the items.

5.   Completion Codes

(i)   Completion code 4 if any formatting or other element
      errors have been made.   One or more items will be
      missing from intfile.

(ii) Completion code 8 if anything is wrong with the
      definition of the files.   FINPUT will not in this
      case process the data.

(iii) Otherwise, the completion code will be 0.

4.2   *UPDATING*

The reader is firstly referred to section 3.3 in the
previous chapter, where there is an introductory discussion
of the updating process.

1.   Command

label UPDATE mainfile updfile newmfile switch ;

label is optional and is any name by which the command can be
      referred.

UPDATE is the name of the file updating program, which updates
      the information in the internal file called mainfile using
      the items in the (different) internal file called updfile
      to form the new contents of the internal file named
      newmfile.

<u>mainfile</u> is an input internal file name, which plays the role
      of main file in the updating process.

<u>updfile</u> is an input internal file name, which plays the role
      of updating file.

<u>newmfile</u> is the name of an output internal file, which plays
      the role of new main file.

<u>switch</u> is replaced by either ON or OFF.   ON protects items
      already in mainfile from alteration in the updating
      process.   OFF allows updating of existing items.

2.   Function and Notes

     There are two aspects to the function of this program.
One is the way in which the program uses the files, and the
other is the process of using one internally formatted item
to modify another and how this affects the preparation of
items for inclusion in updating files.

     We shall start with the first of these - the roles played
by the files.   The result of applying the updating function
to two files, the main file and the updating file, is a third
file, the new main file.   When we say that a modification
takes place to the main file, what we really mean is that when
the process is successfully concluded, there will be a
difference between the main file and the new main file (in
terms of the prototype command, between the contents of
<u>mainfile</u> and <u>newmfile</u>).   We can then talk about updating the
main file regardless of whether it and the new main file
coexist at the end of the process.

     The file used as the updating file (<u>updfile</u>) must be
different from both of the other files (<u>mainfile</u> and <u>newmfile</u>)
If <u>mainfile</u> is a different name from <u>newmfile</u>, both the main
file and the new main file will exist when the updating is
complete.   If <u>mainfile</u> is the same name as <u>newmfile</u>, then
the contents of <u>mainfile</u> will be replaced; the program will
require a work file (see section 3.3) called WORK1 which will
receive the whole updated file before it is copied back to
<u>mainfile</u>, overwriting the previous contents.

     The main file and the updating file must be in ascending
item number sequence (#100).   The following lettered paragraphs describe the way in which UPDATE processes the files.
Each paragraph describes a step taken by the program under
appropriate conditions.   It starts at step A and works down
the list of steps unless instructed otherwise.   The flow-chart
illustrates the same process.

35

Flow-chart of the updating process

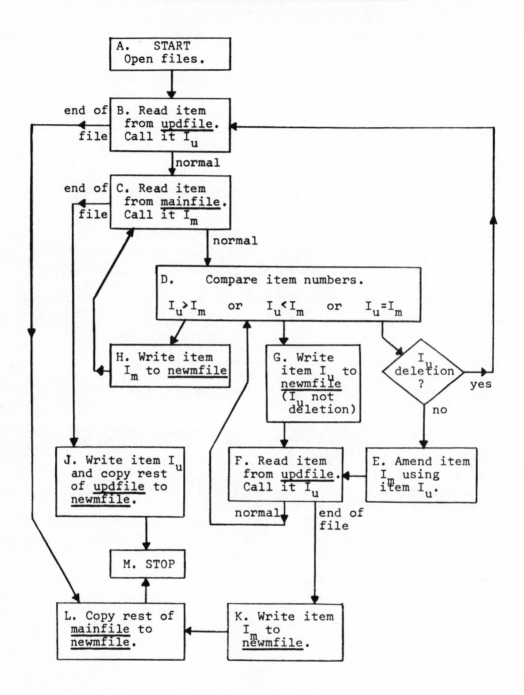

A. Open the files <u>mainfile</u> and <u>updfile</u> so that the "next" item is initially the first item in each.   (This is just to make steps B and C sensible the first time they are executed.)

B. Read the next item from file <u>updfile</u>; call this one I_u. If there were no more items in the file, continue with step L.

C. Read the next item from file <u>mainfile</u>; call this one I_m. If there were no more items in the file, continue with step J.

D. Compare the item numbers of I_u and I_m.   If the item number of I_u comes before that of I_m, continue with step G.   If the item number of I_u comes after that of I_m, continue with step H.   If the items have the same item numbers (which is the only remaining alternative), continue with the next step.

E. If I_u is a deletion item (see note i, below), no item is written into <u>newmfile</u>; continue with step B.   Otherwise, amend the item I_m using I_u, element by element, and proceed to the next step.

F. Read the next item from file <u>updfile</u>; call this one I_u. If there were no more items in the file, continue with step K.   Otherwise, continue with step D.

G. (This step is only done after step D; an addition is made to the main file.)   Unless I_u is a deletion item, write it in normal format into <u>newmfile</u>.   Then continue with step F.

H. (This step is only done after step D; an item in the main file is unaltered.)   Write I_m into <u>newmfile</u>.   Then continue with step C.

J. (This step is only done after step C.)   Write I_u and copy the rest of <u>updfile</u> (except deletion items) into <u>newmfile</u>.   Then continue with step M.

K. (This step is only done after step F.)   Write I_m into <u>newmfile</u>.

L. Copy rest of <u>mainfile</u> to <u>newmfile</u>.

M. Updating done.   Stop.

    This process effectively interfiles the main and updating files in item number sequence but with special action when an item in the updating file has the same number as one in the main file.

Notes

(i) The normal method of updating a file is to prepare an external file containing the new items and amendments to items, use FINPUT to convert it to the internal updating format and then use this file as updating file in an UPDATE command. The external format of deletion items is described near the end of section 3.4. There is a corresponding internal format which is simply equivalent to the instruction "delete item number X" when it is read from an updating file.

(ii) It can be seen from the above description of the updating process (step D) that the only element which participates in the control of it is the item number (#100). Therefore, we must remember that the only method of specifying which item we want amended or deleted is by giving the item number. The LFP System cannot cope directly with requests like "amend Modern Algebra by B.L. van der Waerden as follows . . .".

(iii) The function of switch in the UPDATE command is to enable us to protect items in mainfile from amendment or deletion when newmfile is constructed. Items in updfile which would cause amendment or deletion are ignored if switch is ON. Step E is the relevant step in the program description, and it is executed as it stands if switch is OFF. If switch is ON it is replaced by:

E. Print a warning message and proceed to the next step (i.e. F).

We normally have the switch ON if we intend only to add new items to a file. Then no harm is done if we have made a mistake in an item number in the updating file.

We now move on to the specification of amendments to items in the main file. Items are prepared in the external format containing the item number (element #100) and whichever elements require amendment. There are three possibilities:

(i) An existing element in the main file item is to be changed. In the amendment item (i.e. the item in the updating file with the same item number) we include the replacement element. For example, if item number D2317 has publisher (#900) O.U.P. and we wish to change that to OXFORD to make the item file properly, then we prepare an item as follows:

#100 D2317£ #900 OXFORD£ *

When the amendment is done, the publisher field will be changed and all other elements will be unaltered.

(ii) A new element is to be included in the main file item.
We just include it in the amendment item.

There is a special case which can be illustrated by an
example. Suppose that item number S0314 in the main
file has no author element, that is no element in the
range #601 to #699. If we use some of the LFP System
facilities described later to produce an author
catalogue, this item would be filed according to its
title field. If we wish to include an author in the
item but still have an additional entry in the author
catalogue under its title, we must give the item two
"author" elements, one containing the author, the other
blank. Now, the only way in which a blank element
can be included in one of the element ranges, like
#601 to #699, is to have a non-blank element after
it. So in this example, all we have to do is add a
#602 element to the item, and a blank #601 element
is added automatically for us. The appropriate
amendment item might look like this:

#100 S0314£ #602 KNUTH D.E.£*

(iii) An element is removed from the item in the main file.
This is really a special case of element replacement;
the designated element is replaced by nothing. For
example, to remove the agent code (#200) from item
number D0937, we punch the item

#100 D0937£ #200 £*

"#200" is the tag of a null element.

There is a special situation concerning the ranges of
elements, #401 to #499, #601 to #699, #701 to #799, and #801
to #899, which is related to the case discussed in note (ii)
above. Suppose that item number D1370 has four course codes
(#401 to #404), ABC, DEF, "blank" and GHI. If we remove the
fourth one, GHI, using the item

#100 D1370£ #404 £*

then, because #403 is blank and is no longer followed by a
non-blank element, #403 is also removed automatically and we
are left with two codes, ABC and DEF.

3. Data Definition Cards

Job control cards are required to define the data-sets
associated with mainfile, updfile, and either newmfile, if it
is different from mainfile, or WORK1 if they are the same.

(i) mainfile and updfile are the names of previously
created internal files.

(ii) newmfile is the name of an output file in internal
format. If it is not the same as mainfile, a data-
set must be provided for it with sufficient space
for the updated file.

(iii) WORK1 is the name of the work file used by UPDATE
when mainfile is the same as newmfile. The data-
set associated with it should normally be a temporary
one and should have sufficient space for the updated
file. The catalogued procedure DLFPMCLG (see
Appendix C) provides the user with a work file called
WORK1 which is large enough initially to hold about
5,000 internally formatted items and will expand as
required to a maximum capacity of about 20,000 items.
When the updated file replaces the original version,
the data-set containing mainfile should, of course,
be large enough to accommodate new and enlarged items.

Note.   The new main file, whether it has the name mainfile
or something different, will be written in normal internal
format.

4.   Computer Time

Central processor time for UPDATE depends on the number
of items in mainfile, I_1, and the number of items in updfile,
I_2, as follows.

Time is approximately $0.5+0.001 \times I_1+0.05 \times I_2$ seconds

If, for example, I_1 is 2500 and I_2 is 200, the time
required is about 13 seconds.

If newmfile is the same as mainfile, there is an extra
simple copying operation which takes about 1 second per 1000
items.

5.   Completion Codes

(i) Completion code 4 is set in the following circumstances.

Any #101 element is encountered. The #101 element
specifies a change of item number, which might cause
the new main file to be out of sequence, so the user
is warned about it.

The following are considered minor errors. Processing
continues after appropriate action has been taken.

An amendment made an item too large (see section 3.4).
The amendment item is ignored.

A deletion or amendment is attempted when switch is
ON. The amendment item is ignored.

Two or more items with the same item number (#100)
occur in updfile which are not amendment items.
The second and subsequent items with that number
are ignored.   Note that it is permitted to have
several amendment items with the same item number.
They will be applied one after the other to the
same item.

(ii)   Completion code 8 is set in either of the following
cases.

The files are not properly defined.   UPDATE then
does no work.

Items with the same item number are found in
mainfile.   Processing stops and mainfile is
unchanged.

(iii)   Completion code 12 is set if any items are faulty
in the files.

This cannot usually happen as a result of a user's
error.   The main file is not changed.

(iv)   Otherwise the completion code will be 0.

4.3   *COPYING FILES*

1.   Command

   label FCOPY   infile select outfile ;

label is optional and is any name by which the command can
   be referred.

FCOPY is the name of the internal format file copying program
   which reads items from the internal file infile, applies
   the tests specified in select and writes the items which
   pass the tests into the internal file outfile.

infile is an input internal file name, from which items are
   copied.

select is a string of no more than 128 characters (including
   the blanks), enclosed in quote characters.   There are
   certain syntax rules for the contents of the string
   which enable it to be interpreted as a condition for
   selection of internally formatted items.   There is a
   way to ask for the selection parameter to be ignored,
   so that the copy is total.

outfile is the name of an output internal file, into which
   selected items are written.

41

2.   Function and Notes

The basic action of the FCOPY program is very simple;
items are read from an internal file (infile) and selectively
written, unchanged, to the internal file outfile.   If the
select string is completely blank or is empty, that is if
select is either

                    ' ',   or   '',

then no selection takes place and all the items are written
into outfile.

Notes

(i)   The items on outfile will be in the same sequence as
       they occurred in infile.

(ii)   No item will be changed in any way. If the file infile
       is in updating format, then the copied items in outfile
       will also be in updating format.

(iii) The file names infile and outfile may be the same. In
       that case, the work file WORK1 will be required.   The
       program will do a selective copy from infile to WORK1
       and then a simple total copy back again, overwriting the
       previous contents of infile. This facility can be used,
       instead of an update with deletions, to remove from a
       file items with certain characteristics.

       If the request is to copy a file to itself unselectively,
       the program will not bother to do it.*

(iv)   The facilities available for selection and the syntax of
       the select string are also used by other programs in the
       system and, for that reason, are described in detail in
       the next section of this chapter (section 4.4).

       At this point we just list the fields within the item
       that can be used for selection.

                    #100, item number;
                    #102, type code;
                    #200, agent code
                    #203, agent report code;
                    #300, status code
                    #400, the course codes,
                            range #401 to #499.

       For example, we can select items which were ordered from
       A. Gent Ltd. (#200) and have not yet arrived (#300) and
       for which the expected arrival date is in June (#203).

---

* But this does not answer the question "can machines think?".

3.   Data Definition Cards

   Job control cards are required to define the data-sets
to hold the files infile and outfile, if it is different
from infile, or WORK1, otherwise.

   (i)   infile is the name of a previously created internal
         file.

   (ii)   outfile is the name of an output file in internal
          format.   If it is different from infile, a data-set
          must be provided (extant or new) with sufficient
          space for the copied items.   It will certainly be
          no larger than infile.

   (iii)   WORK1 is the name of the internal work file used
           when outfile is the same as infile.   The catalogued
           procedure DLFPMCLG (see Appendix C) provides a file
           called WORK1 with a maximum capacity of about 20,000
           items.

4.   Computer Time

   Central processor time for FCOPY depends on the number
of items in infile, the complexity of the selection specification and the number of items written to outfile.   Often,
the more complex the selection is, the fewer items will be
selected for outfile.

   On the assumption that there are about 100 characters
per item in the variable length elements, the fastest copy
is an unselective one at a rate of about 700 items per second.
If the copy is selective, the rate will nearly always be more
than 500 items read from infile per second.

   If infile is the same as outfile, the selected items
will be copied back from WORK1 at about 1,000 per second.

5.   Completion Codes

   (i)   Completion code 4 is set if the user violates the
         rules for constructing select in Section 4.4.   The
         copy will be done but the selection may not be
         what was desired.

   (ii)   Completion code 8 is set by more serious errors in
          select and by errors in defining the files.   No
          copying is done.

   (iii)   Completion code 12 is set if infile contains a
           faultily formatted item.   This is not usually
           the result of any user error.

   (iv)   Otherwise the completion code is set to 0.

4.4   *SELECTION OF ITEMS FROM FILES*

The LFP System has a sequential selection mechanism of limited scope. It is sequential because it operates only while reading a file sequentially. It can only be used on internally formatted files and its function is to either select items for processing or ignore them, according to the values of certain of their elements. The principal programs which use selection are FCOPY, which copies internal files, and PRINT, which produces formatted lists of items from internal files. If we wish to apply a selection criterion, we provide a string of characters which is interpreted as a selection specification. This section describes the facility and the rules for constructing a selection specification.

1.   Syntax of Selection Specifications

A selection specification has one of the following forms. Either

' test '

or

' test & test & . . . '

In other words, it is either a single test or more than one test separated by the & character. Spaces or commas may intervene.

Notes

(i)   A specification can be all blank or it can be of zero length (i.e. contain no characters at all), in which case all items will be selected because no tests will be applied.

(ii)   The total length of the specification string, including all spaces and commas, must not exceed 128 characters. If it does, it is first chopped off after the 128th character and then the last test is removed if it is not syntactically correct.

test specifies a comparison to be made with each item, and takes the following form:

tag relation value

Spaces or commas may separate the three components.

tag is either   #number

or just   number

No spaces or commas are allowed in tag.

44

number is one of the following three digit numbers (they
are element numbers, of course):

> 100
> 102
> 200
> 203
> 300
> 400

relation is one of the following symbols:

> = (read "equal")
> ¬= (read "not equal")
> ¬ (read "not"; and exactly equivalent to ¬=)

value is one or more characters which may be any except &,
space and comma. The length of value is restricted
when the element number is either 100, 200 or 400, as
follows:

> 100, length restricted to no more than 5 characters
>
> 200 and 400, length restricted to no more than 3
> characters.

2. Interpretation of Selection Specifications

We shall refer to the various components described in
the paragraphs on syntax above using the underlined symbolic
names. Items are read from a file sequentially, and normally
passed directly to the processing program. If, however, a
selection specification is in effect, each item is tested
using the test's and only those that "satisfy" are passed to
the program.

The result of applying a test to an item is either "true"
or "false". If the selection specification consists of just
one test, then an item is selected if the result is true but
not if the result is false. If there are several test's
separated by & characters, an item is selected only if the
results of the test's are all true.

We now describe how the result of a test is obtained
when applied to an item in a file.

(i) When number is either 102, 203 or 300, the result
depends on the value of one of the one-character
coded elements, #102 (type), #203 (agent report) or
#300 (status).

If relation is =, the result is true if the element
is one of the characters in value and false otherwise.

45

If <u>relation</u> is either ⌐= or ⌐, the result is true
if <u>the element</u> is not the same as any of the characters in <u>value</u> and false otherwise.

So we can say, for example, the status must be none
of the following: A, J, X or Y.

    #300⌐=AJXY

Another example: The type code is either B or J.

    102=BJ

(ii)   When <u>number</u> is 100 or 200, selection is by element
#100 (item number) or #200 (agent code).   There
will be up to 5 characters in <u>value</u> if <u>number</u> is
100, or up to 3 if it is 200, and if <u>value is</u>
shorter than these maxima the comparison will be
limited to however many characters are given.

For example, those items whose numbers begin with
letter D can be selected, or rejected, using

    #100=D   or   #100⌐=D

(iii)   When <u>number</u> is 400, the result depends on elements
in the range #401 to #499.   Let the length of <u>value</u>
be n characters; n will be either 1, 2 or 3.   The
comparisons will be between <u>value</u> and the first n
characters of the elements.

If <u>relation</u> is =, the result is true only if the
first n characters of at least one of the #401 to
#499 range elements agree with <u>value</u>.

If <u>relation</u> is ⌐= or ⌐, the result is true only if
the first n characters of each of the elements differ
from <u>value</u>.

For example, if we had chosen the codes in such a
way that the first letter indicated a department,
we might select items for mathematics courses by
including the <u>test</u>

    #400=M

As an illustration of how to combine criteria for
selecting items from a file, let us construct a selection
specification for getting all the items in a file which are
not monographs and which have Geography department course
codes and have not yet arrived from the agents.

The assumptions are that monographs have type code B (#102), that Geography codes start with the letter G and that status codes A and C both refer to orders not yet received.

To select non-monographs, we need

    #102¬=B

To select Geography department material, we need

    #400=G

For non-arrivals, we need

    #300=AC

All three of these must be true for the items which we want, so the complete selection specification is

    '#102¬=B & #300=AC & #400=G'

Note that the order in which the test's are written does not matter.

SORTING

BIBLIOGRAPHIC

FILES

5

In Chapter 4, the programs for file maintenance were
described and it was pointed out that the central one, UPDATE,
requires that the files upon which it operates are in one
particular sequence, namely by item number.   Apart from
maintenance, however, we have little use for the item number
sequence; we are far more interested in having the items in
author, class number or title order, for example.   Sorting
a file is the process of putting its items into a predefined
sequence which may be entirely different from the original.

In the LFP System, there are three programs concerned
with file sequence:

(i)   SORT accepts a file in any sequence and arranges its
      items in a specified one.

(ii) MERGE reads two files, assumed sorted in a specified
      sequence, and interfiles them to form a third file
      consisting of all the items from each of the original
      files.

(iii) CHKSRT reads a file and reports on whether it is in
      a specified sequence.

There are two aspects to each of these processes.   The
first is the sequencing or filing arrangement, and the second
is the management of the files involved.   In the LFP System
these are separated in the programming.   SORT, MERGE and
CHKSRT are mainly file management programs and, in theory,
virtually any arrangement can be "plugged into" them.   Nine
filing arrangements are currently implemented in the LFP
System and can be used with all three programs.

5.1   *SEQUENCING ROUTINES*

For any desired filing arrangement, a subroutine can be
written for the computer, which accepts two items and decides
which one should precede the other in the sequence.   The
rules for arrangement must, of course, be absolutely precise.
We do not describe how to write such a subroutine in this
manual; it is a programmer's job.   Such routines are suitable
for use with all three of the main programs.

The sequencing routines currently available in the LFP
System are shown in the table of figure 5.1.   In most cases,

the sequencing field, which determines an item's position in the file, is simply the concatenation of some of the elements of the item.   If an element is absent from the item it is usually replaced in the sequencing field by one or more blank characters, which file before all the others. The exceptions are the author and title elements (#601 and #701); if either of these are absent, it is just omitted from the sequencing field.   So, for example, if SEQ601 is used and an item has no author element, it will be filed under its title.

Sequencing Routine Name	Sequencing Field (How constructed)		Additional items gene- rated for SORT
SEQ100	#100	(item number)	
SEQ200	#200+#900+#601+#701	(agent,publisher)	
SEQ467	#401+#601+#701	(course,author)	in #400 range
SEQ476	#401+#701+#601	(course,title)	in #400 range
SEQ486	#401+#801+#601+#701	(course,class)	in #400 range
SEQ601	#601+#701	(author,title)	in #600 range
SEQ701	#701+#601	(title,author)	in #700 range
SEQ801	#801+#601+#701	(class,author)	in #800 range
SEQ900	#900+#601+#701	(publisher,author)	

Figure 5.1   Table of Sequencing Routines

Additional Entries

     Where indicated in the right hand column of figure 5.1, sequencing routines can generate additional items during the first phase of the SORT program.   These additional items are then included in the final sorted file in the appropriate positions.   So we can arrange for any item to appear in more than one place in certain sequences.

     Additional entries are generated in sequences where the primary filing field is the first element in one of the ranges #401 to #499, #601 to #699, #701 to #799 or #801 to #899, and an item has more than one element in that range.   An extra entry is produced for each element, after the first in the range, which is present in the item up to the last non-blank

one.   In these additional items, all elements other than
those in the range are the same as in the original item.
The elements in the range concerned will be a permutation
of the elements in the main item.

Comparison Operations

When two sequencing fields have been assembled, they
are compared to see which "comes first" in a file.   The
comparison is, in all the provided sequencing routines, a
simple character comparison.   The routines work along the
two fields together from left to right until they come to
a difference in the fields, which can be of two types.

(i)   One field is shorter than the other, and the routine
has come to the end of it.   The shorter field then
comes first.

(ii)   The difference is between the two characters in
corresponding positions in the two fields.   The
field containing the "lower" character comes first.
The table in figure 3.1 of Chapter 3 shows the
collating convention.   Briefly, it is that special
characters come before letters which come before
numerals

Sample Comparisons

The symbol ∧ is used to show where the first different
character occurs.

(i)   HOMER   comes before
TOLSTOY
∧

(ii)   MORPHEUS   comes before
MORROW
∧

(iii)   ANIMALS   comes before
ANIMALS IN THE FARM

The difference occurs when the end of the first
field is reached.

(iv)   ANIMAL WORSHIP   comes before
ANIMALS
∧

(v)   'PARADISE LOST'   comes well before
PARADISE LOST
∧

5.2 *SORTING INTERNAL FILES*

1.   Command

   label SORT infile sortfile sequence ;

label is optional and is any name by which the command can
      be referred.

SORT is the name of the program which reads an internal
      file, infile, and sorts the items into the sequence
      determined by sequence, writing them into the
      internally formatted file sortfile.

infile is the name of an input internal file containing,
      in any sequence, the items to be sorted.

sortfile is the name of an output internal file into which
      the items from infile will be written in the specified
      sequence.   It may contain additional items, generated
      by the sequencing routine.

sequence is the name of a sequencing routine.   That is one
      of the names listed in figure 5.1.

2.   Function and Notes

   The function of program SORT is to arrange the items in
an internal file, infile, in the order determined by the
operation of the sequencing routine, sequence.   The sorted
file is written into sortfile which is usually, but does not
have to be, different from infile.

   If sortfile is the same as infile, the sorted file will
replace the unsorted one.

   The items will be unchanged, but some additional ones
may be generated as described in section 5.1.

3.   Data Definition Cards

   Job control cards are required to define the data-sets
associated with infile and sortfile, if it is different
from infile.   SORT also uses four work files called WORK1,
WORK2, WORK3 and WORK4;   they are all internal files.

   (i)   infile is the name of a previously created internal
         file.

   (ii) sortfile is the name of an output file in internal
         format.   If it is different from infile, a data-set
         must be provided with sufficient space for all the
         items in infile plus, possibly, some additional
         entries.

(iii)   WORK1, WORK2, WORK3 and WORK4 are the names of the
        work files required by SORT.   Data-sets must always
        be provided for these files.   The catalogued pro-
        cedure DLFPMCLG (see Appendix C) provides for a file
        called WORK1 with a maximum capacity of about 20,000
        items.   The space requirements are about the same
        for each of the work files.   A typical quantity for
        each one would be $\frac{3}{4}$ of the space occupied by infile,
        but this will depend in a non-linear way on the number
        of items in sortfile.   The most that will be required
        is the space of sortfile.   Use the following method
        to calculate the space.

        Suppose that infile occupies t tracks on a 2314 disk
        (see Section 4.1).

        Let s be the nearest whole number to $\frac{3t}{4}$, and let

        i be the nearest whole number to the value of $\frac{t}{12}$.

        If either s or i is zero, increase it to 1.

        Put SPACE=(TRK,(s,i)) on the DD cards for the work
        files.

4.   Computer Time

        Central processor time for SORT depends on the number of
items written into sortfile and on the complexity of the
sequencing routine.   SORT is one of the most time-consuming
operations, so it is important to be able to estimate the time.
If the number of items in sortfile is N and the complexity of
the routine is represented by a number C, the time requirement
is approximately

                    C x N x L seconds,

where L is, mathematically speaking, the ceiling of $\log_2 N$
and some values are shown below.

N in the range	L	N in the range	L
5- 8	3	513- 1024	10
9- 16	4	1025- 2048	11
17- 32	5	2049- 4096	12
33- 64	6	4097- 8192	13
65-128	7	8193-16384	14
129-256	8	16385-32768	15
257-512	9	32769-65536	16

Figure 5.2   Table of ceiling of $\log_2 N$

The values of C for the sequencing routines in figure 5.1 are estimated as follows:

Sequencing Routines	C
SEQ100	0.0021
SEQ200, SEQ900	0.0050
SEQ467, SEQ476	0.0044
SEQ486	0.0052
SEQ601, SEQ701	0.0039
SEQ801	0.0051

Example

Sort a file of 2400 items into author sequence, using SEQ601, assuming that sortfile will contain 2500 items.

$N=2500$, $C=0.0039$, $L=12$ (from the table)

Time required is about 2500x0.0039x12 = 117 seconds.

5.   Completion Codes

(i)   Completion code 4 is set if infile is empty.   sortfile will not be changed.

(ii)   Completion code 8 is set if any of the files, including the four work files, are not properly defined. sortfile will not be changed (even if it is defined).

(iii) Completion code 12 is set if any item is faulty.   This will not usually be due to any error on the part of the user.

(iv)   Otherwise the completion code will be 0.

5.3   MERGING INTERNAL FILES

1.   Command

label MERGE fileone filetwo outfile sequence ;

label is optional and is any name by which the command can be
       referred.

MERGE is the name of the program which reads two sorted
   files, fileone and filetwo, in internal format and
   merges the items into one sorted file, outfile.

fileone is the name of an input internal file, assumed to
   be already in the sequence determined by sequence.

filetwo is the name of an input internal file, different
   from fileone and assumed to be already in the sequence
   determined by sequence.

outfile is the name of an output file in internal format,
   which will contain all the items from both fileone
   and filetwo in the sequence determined by sequence.

sequence is the name of a sequencing routine; one of the
   names listed in figure 5.1.

2.   Function and Notes

   The MERGE program reads two files in internal format
and combines them to form a third file which contains all
the items from the original two, unchanged, without additional items and in the sequence determined by sequence.
MERGE assumes that the two input files, fileone and filetwo,
are already in the sequence determined by that same
sequencing routine.

   For example, if AUTHOR1 and AUTHOR2 are the names of
two files, both of which are sorted in author sequence
(using SEQ601), the command required to merge them into
one file, AUTHOR3, is:

          MERGE AUTHOR1 AUTHOR2 AUTHOR3 SEQ601;

   Normally, three distinct files will be involved, but
it is possible to have outfile the same as either fileone
or filetwo and in that case MERGE writes the combined file
first to the work file WORK1 and simply copies it back to
the designated file.

   The file names fileone and filetwo must be different.
That is, you cannot merge a file with itself.

   The items will not be changed in any way as they are
copied to outfile.   An implication of this is that if
either fileone or filetwo, but not both, is in updating
format, then outfile may be in updating format as a whole,
yet possibly be unsuitable for updating.

3.   Data Definition Cards

   Job control cards are required to define the data-sets
associated with files fileone, filetwo and, if it is
different from both of those, outfile.   If outfile is the

same as either <u>fileone</u> or <u>filetwo</u>, then a data-set will be required for WORK1, a work file.

(i)   <u>fileone</u> is the name of a previously created internal <u>file</u>.

(ii)   <u>filetwo</u> is the name of a previously created internal <u>file</u>.

(iii) <u>outfile</u> is the name of an output internal file. The data-set must be large enough to hold all the items from both <u>fileone</u> and <u>filetwo</u>. The sum of the spaces occupied by those two files will certainly be sufficient for <u>outfile</u>.

(iv)   WORK1 is the name of a work file in internal format. The space allowance must be as for <u>outfile</u> above. It is only required when <u>outfile</u> is the same as either <u>fileone</u> or <u>filetwo</u> and whichever it is should, of course, be large enough to receive the resulting file. The catalogued procedure DLFPMCLG (see Appendix C) provides a work file WORK1 with a maximum capacity of about 20,000 items.

4.   Computer Time

Central processor time for MERGE depends on the sum of the number of items in files <u>fileone</u> and <u>filetwo</u> and on the complexity of the sequencing routine. If the total number of items involved is N and the complexity of the sequencing routine is represented by K, the time requirement is approximately

$$K \times N \text{ seconds}$$

The values of K for the sequencing routines in figure 5.1 are estimated as follows:

Sequencing Routines	K
SEQ100	0.0025
SEQ200, SEQ900 SEQ486, SEQ801	0.0050
SEQ467, SEQ476 SEQ601, SEQ701	0.0039

The time could be significantly reduced if K is large (i.e. <u>sequence</u> is complex) and one of the input files is exhausted well before the other one.

If WORK1 is used, a simple copying operation is done at the end of the process, which takes about 1 second for every 1,000 items.

Example

To merge two files of 2,500 items each in author sequence, using SEQ601 takes about

$$0.0039 \times 5000 = 19.5 \text{ seconds}$$

5. Completion Codes

(i) Completion code 4 is not set by MERGE under any circumstances.

(ii) Completion code 8 is set if any of the files, including WORK1 if required, are not properly defined or if an illegal combination of files is specified. The merge does not take place and outfile, if defined, is unchanged.

(iii) Completion code 12 is set if any item is faulty. This will not usually result from any user error.

(iv) Otherwise the completion code will be 0.

5.4 *CHECKING SEQUENCES IN INTERNAL FILES*

1. Command

label CHKSRT infile sequence ;

label is optional and is any name by which the command can be referred.

CHKSRT is the name of the program which reads an internal file, infile, and checks that it is in the sequence determined by a sequencing routine, sequence.

infile is the name of an input internal file, which is read and checked by CHKSRT.

sequence is the name of a sequencing routine; one of the names listed in figure 5.1.

2. Function and Notes

The function of program CHKSRT is simply to read the internal file, infile, and apply the sequencing routine, sequence, to every pair of adjacent items in the file to see whether the file is in the sequence specified. The program reports the result of the check both in printed form and in the completion code.

·   If the file is in sequence, the completion code is set to 0.

If the file is empty, that is if there are no items at all in it, the completion code is set to 4.

If the file is not in sequence, processing stops at the point where this condition is detected, an indication is given of where it happens and the completion code is set to 6.

In all cases, an appropriate message is printed out and in no case will the file infile be altered.   As will be seen later, the completion code returned by a command can be used to control the execution of other commands, so that we can say, for example, "see if file A is in author sequence and if it is not, then sort it into author sequence".

3.   Data Definition Card

A job control card is required to associate a data-set with file infile, which is the name of a previously created internal file.

4.   Computer Time

Central processor time for CHKSRT depends on the number of items read, which may be less than the total number of items in infile, and the complexity of the sequencing routine, sequence.   When submitting a job we must, of course, allow for the reading of the whole file.   Let N be the number of items in the file and let the number S represent the complexity of sequence.   The time required will be approximately

$$S \times N \text{ seconds}$$

The values of S for the sequencing routines in figure 5.1 are estimated as follows:

Sequencing Routines	S
SEQ100	0.0013
SEQ200, SEQ900 SEQ486, SEQ801	0.0035
SEQ467, SEQ476 SEQ601, SEQ701	0.0030

Example

To check a file of 2,500 items for author sequence using
SEQ601 takes about

$$0.003 \times 2500 = 7.5 \text{ seconds}$$

5.   Completion Codes

Some of these are described in the description of the
function of the program.

(i)   Completion code 0 is set if the file <u>infile</u> is in
specified sequence.

(ii)   Completion code 4 is set if the file <u>infile</u> is empty.
This situation may or may not be regarded as successful.

(iii)   Completion code 6 is set if the file <u>infile</u> is not
in the specified sequence.

(iv)   Completion code 8 is set if the file <u>infile</u> is not
properly defined.   No checking is done.

(v)   Completion code 12 is set if a faulty item is
encountered.   This is usually not a result of an
error by the user.

Printing is one of the primary functions of the Library File Processing System; there would be little point in maintaining and sorting files on magnetic disks if there were no way of displaying them visually for the benefit of library users and library staff. In the present system, display is restricted to lists produced on a high speed line-printer with the 60 characters shown in figure 3.1. Within this restriction, however, the printing facility is quite versatile, and the user of the system has moderately fine control over the appearance of the printed information.

One program is responsible for printing out internal files, namely PRINT. The program is invoked by a command which must also give the whereabouts of a set of printing instructions, or "print-control statements", prepared by the user. Broadly speaking, these instructions specify three types of information for program PRINT.

(i) The internal file, or files, to be printed.

(ii) Which items are to be included; that is an optional selection criterion.

(iii) In the printed items, which elements are to be included and how they are to be formatted.

The instructions must be contained in a card file and may, therefore, either be included in the job on punched cards or be prestored on a disk and read by PRINT from there. The user has the facility to modify his requirements easily and as often as necessary. In this chapter, we first have a description of the command, PRINT, and then an explanation of the use of the printing instructions.

6.1   *PRINT COMMAND*

1.   Command

   <u>label</u> PRINT <u>cardfile</u> <u>column</u> ;

<u>label</u> is optional and is any name by which the command can be referred.

PRINT is the name of the file printing program, which reads print-control statements from the card file called <u>cardfile</u> and prints the contents of internal files as specified in those statements.

cardfile is an input card file name. The file should
     contain print-control statements to specify which
     internal files are to be printed, and how. This
     file is called the "control file".

column is a number which should not exceed 80. Columns
     beyond that card column in the records (or cards)
     of cardfile will be ignored. That is, the print-
     control statements will be read from columns 1 to
     column inclusive in cardfile. The usual values
     of column in practice are 80 (for whole cards) and
     72 (for numbered cards).

2.   Function and Notes

     The program PRINT operates in two main phases. The
first reads instructions for printing, or print-control statements, from a control file whose name is cardfile. The types
of statement and their various forms are discussed in section
6.2. If the statements are syntactically valid and not
obviously nonsense, the second phase of PRINT is executed and
the formatted lists are produced, normally on a line-printer.
It is then possible to go back to the first phase and read
another set of statements and print more lists, and so on, all
within one invocation of PRINT.

     The control file, cardfile, should not be confused with
the internal file or files containing the items to be printed.
The name(s) of the latter will be included in the statements
contained in cardfile. Also, cardfile may contain a reference
to another card file containing further print-control statements.

     There now follow some notes on the way in which PRINT uses
control files. For this purpose, we have a simple description
of a control file without going into detail.

     Firstly, a "set of instructions" consists of all that is
needed to specify a listing; it contains

   (i)   One or more input internal file names,

  (ii)   Optionally, a selection specification, which is
         applied to all items read from the internal files,

 (iii)   Element formatting instructions.

     An "execute" statement is one which, following a set of
instructions, signals the end of them. It also specifies what
is to be done after the files have been printed; there are
three possibilities.

   (i)   Terminate PRINT,

  (ii)   Read another set of instructions from this control
         file,

(iii)   Switch to another (named) control file and read
another set of instructions from there.

A control file consists of one or more sets of instructions, each followed by an execute statement.   PRINT starts
by reading the first set of instructions in cardfile,
printing the specified lists, and then proceeds to further
sets of instructions as directed by the execute statements.

Note that, in general, once instructions and execute
statements in a control file have been read,
whereupon PRINT is terminated or another control
file switched in, further reading of it at any
stage in the same job step can only occur if it
is stored on a disk (i.e. not on punched cards
submitted with the job) and even then it can only
be read from the beginning again.   There is an
exception; a special card file called CONTROL
can be read in sections at different stages either
during the execution of one command or during the
whole job step.

3.   Data Definition Cards

Job control cards are required to define the data-sets
associated with cardfile and any other control files and all
internal files referred to in the control files that are read
by PRINT.   There is a decoding facility, described in
section 6.2, which requires the definition of a specially
organized file of codes called SYSCODE.   This is only needed
if the decoding facility is actually used in the job step.
A description of how to construct a file of codes can be
found in Chapter 8.

   (i)   cardfile and other control files are card files and
can be on punched cards submitted with the job or
in data-sets previously created on a disk.

  (ii)   All internal files are previously created files.

(iii)   SYSCODE is a previously created file of codes.

4.   Computer Time

Central processor time will depend, for each listing
operation in the control file(s), on the number of items read
from the internal file(s), the complexity of the selection
criterion, the number of items printed and the complexity of
the formatting.   No attempt will be made to give a formula.
Assuming that items have about 100 characters of variable
length information each, then PRINT can be expected to format
about 50 items per second for printing in the worst cases.

5. Completion Codes

  (i) Completion code 4 is set if suspected errors are detected in a control file.

 (ii) Completion code 8 is set if errors are found in a control file or if any required file is not defined properly. Affected lists will not be printed.

(iii) Otherwise the completion code will be 0.

6.2 *PRINT-CONTROL STATEMENTS*

    Program PRINT is controlled by sets of instructions entered in card files (control files). As described in the previous section (6.1), one invocation of PRINT can interpret several sets of instructions. In this section, we describe how to construct a set of instructions. Each set of instructions consists of an appropriate combination of the following types of statement.

  (i) List statements specify which internal files are to be printed. Any number of files can be specified.

 (ii) The Select statement is used to include a selection specification which applies to all the files mentioned in the list statements.

(iii) Heading statements are used to insert a line of text within each printed item and to print elements as headings for groups of items instead of with each item.

 (iv) Format statements determine which elements are printed and in what position in the item.

  (v) Execute statements, one of which must come at the end of each set of instructions, stop the interpretation phase of PRINT and specify what is to be done when the corresponding printing is complete.

1. General Considerations

    The instructions are initially key-punched onto 80-column cards; later a copy may be stored in a card file on a disk. The first thing to decide is whether the whole card is going to be used for instructions or whether some columns at the end of the card will be used for card numbering. (Note that if it is intended to have PRINT read the instructions from the

special file called CONTROL, the last eight columns will
always be ignored - the user has no choice.) This decision
made, the print-control statements can be placed on the
cards unformatted, i.e. without earmarking columns for
particular portions of the statements or restricting a
statement to one card only or a card to one statement only.

Now some general rules and definitions for the construction of print-control statements.

  (i)   The characters permitted are the 60 listed in
        figure 3.1, Chapter 3.

 (ii)   A special symbol is one of the characters
        ; ( ) + #   These have special significance.

(iii)   A string is a sequence of characters.   Any
        character or combination of characters may
        occur in a string.   Ordinary numbers and
        English words (in capitals, of course) are
        examples of string.   Strings punched on
        cards must be separated from each other, for
        the PRINT program must recognize the begin-
        ning and end of a string.   Spaces, commas
        and special symbol's are used to separate
        string's and we therefore need a way of
        delimiting a string which contains any of
        these characters.   Single quotes (') are
        placed one at each end of the string, for
        example

                 '#300=BD & #102=J'

        The quotes are not included in the internal
        representation of the string.   We might wish
        to write a string with an apostrophe in it,
        and we do this by placing two adjacent quotes
        wherever we want one apostrophe and enclosing
        the string in quotes, for example we punch

                 'JOHN''S'

        to get the string JOHN'S into the computer.

 (iv)   A comment is any sequence of characters
        starting with the character-pair /* and ending
        with the character-pair */.   These pairs are
        regarded as composite symbols and the two
        characters must be in adjacent card columns.
        A comment is syntactically equivalent to a
        space and is therefore, in most contexts,
        ignored.   It can be used to incorporate
        comments in the set of instructions which
        are for the benefit of the human reader and
        ignored by the computer.

(v) Commas and <u>comment</u>'s are syntactically inter-
changeable with spaces and wherever one space
may occur, any number of spaces may occur.
So any sequence of spaces, commas and <u>comment</u>'s
is equivalent to one space as far as interpretation of the statements is concerned.

To illustrate the above general remarks, we give a short
sample set of instructions as they might appear on punched
cards.

```
                                            Column 73
                                            v
        /* THIS IS A SAMPLE */              00000010
 LIST FILE AF01; /* AF01 IS IN AUTHOR ORDER */ 00000020
 SELECT ITEMS IF '#300=BD'; /* ON THE SHELF */ 00000030
5,(#601 /*AUTHOR*/,5,#701 /*TITLE*/),       00000040
     CONTINUE IN 15;                        00000050
 END; /* EXECUTE, THEN TERMINATE PRINT */   00000060
```

The interpretation of the statements will be explained
later.   At this stage we make the following notes.

(i) Columns 73 to 80 of each card are used for a card
number and PRINT must be instructed to ignore them.

(ii) The example is rich in comments.   In practice one
would rarely use so many.

(iii) PRINT encounters <u>string</u>'s and <u>special symbol</u>'s in
the statement on cards 40 and 50 in the following
order:

```
     5   (   #        601    5   #
     701  )  CONTINUE        IN  15   ;
```

(iv) Comments apart, the example is verbose from the
computer's point of view and could be rendered:

```
LIST AF01; SELECT IF '#300=BD';        00000010
5 (#601, 5, #701) 15; END;             00000020
```

Several of the <u>string</u>'s are "noise" words, without
meaning for the machine but, like the comments,
making the instructions more comprehensible to the
human user.

2.   Print-Control Statement Structure

When the interpreter section of program PRINT starts to
read a statement, it examines the <u>string</u>'s and <u>special symbol</u>'
from left to right until it finds one which tells it what type
of statement is has to interpret.   Continuing its scan to the
right, PRINT then looks for further information, the nature of

which depends on the identified statement type. A semicolon
(which is one of the special symbol's) signifies the end of
the statement and, unless it is an execute statement, PRINT
then proceeds to the next statement. The string's which
determine statement type are certain keywords, like LIST,
SELECT and END in the example above, and numbers. The special
symbol's (+ and # encountered while PRINT is trying to
identify the statement type tell the program that the statement is a format statement.

The implication of this method of interpreting statements
is that noise words can be inserted at various places and are
ignored by the program simply because they are not what the
program is looking for. We can, for example, put anything at
the beginning of the statement and it will be ignored unless
it is an identifying keyword or one of the things which
indicates a format statement.

The ability to include noise can be confusing at first
and so in this chapter we describe the statement types using
a "recommended" form which, although concise, is not the
briefest possible but is reasonably easy to read and under-
stand. In the paragraphs that follow, the statements are
described with the help of a simple notation. Statement
prototypes are written as sequences of words and symbols.
Strings in capital letters and the symbols

; ( ) + #

are punched as they stand. Underlined words in lower case
are, as usual, symbolic names for strings supplied by the user
in each particular application. In most of the statements,
alternative forms are allowed and this is indicated in the
prototypes by writing alternatives one above the other and
connecting them with a brace (}) on the right. Sometimes,
part of a statement may be omitted at the user's discretion.
In the prototype statements, strings and symbols within brackets
([ ]) are optional. Neither the braces nor the brackets are
to be included in real statements. Strings must be separated
from each other by a space or its equivalent. A special symbol
need not be separated from either string's or other special
symbol's, although it would not be an error if it were.

3.   List Statement

Prototype

        LIST ⎫ FILE filename   ⎫
                                           ⎬ ;
        PRINT ⎭ FILES (filename . . .) ⎭

   (i) filename stands for an internal file name. The user
        may assign different values to each occurrence of the
        symbol filename.

(ii)   The ellipses (. . .) can be replaced by as many
       further file names as required.

(iii) The keyword alternatives (LIST and PRINT) have
       exactly the same meaning.

Examples

               LIST FILE AF01;
               PRINT FILE XYZ;
               LIST FILES (LBK SBK MBK);
               PRINT FILES (TOM, TOM);

Function

       The list statement tells program PRINT which internal
file or files it is to print.   If a parenthesized list of
files is given, the program will work through the files in
the order in which they occur in the statement.   The files
in such a list need not be different (see the fourth
example) and this provides a simple technique for getting
more than one copy of a listing.

Placement

       List statements can be placed anywhere in a set of
instructions, and the user is not restricted to one list
statement per set.   All the file names mentioned in list
statements throughout a set of instructions are gathered
into one list of names.

Note that a set of instructions must contain at least one
       list statement.

4.   Select Statement

Prototype

$$\text{SELECT ITEMS} \quad \left.\begin{matrix} \text{IF} \\ \\ \text{WHEN} \end{matrix}\right\} \quad \underline{select} \; ;$$

       select is a string whose length should not exceed
128 characters.   The content of select is a selection
specification as described in section 4.4.   If spaces
or special characters are contained it must be enclosed
in quotes.

Examples

               SELECT ITEMS IF 300=BDF;

               SELECT ITEMS WHEN '#102=X & #400=A';

Function

The select statement specifies a selection criterion
to be applied to the items from all the files mentioned in
list statements in the current set of instructions. **Refer**
to section 4.4 for a description of the selection mechanism
and facilities. If a set of instructions contains no
select statement, all items read from the files are printed.

Placement

A set of instructions may have no more than one select
statement and it does not matter where it occurs in the set.
The user is not obliged to include a select statement.

5.   Space Statement

Prototype

SPACE <u>lines</u> **;**

<u>lines</u> is a number between 0 and 30 inclusive.

Example

SPACE 2;

Function

The space statement specifies to program PRINT the number
of clear lines which are to separate printed items.   <u>lines</u>
completely blank lines will be inserted between items.   If
there is no space statement, the assumption will be **SPACE 0;**
Each item will be started on a new line.

Note

Printer stationery is continuous with perforation every
11 inches.   We divide output into pages by leaving a few
blank lines on each side of the perforation and can then print
60 lines on each page.   Program PRINT will automatically
avoid splitting an item at the perforation and rather leave
a few extra lines blank at the bottom of a page and start the
item at the top of the next page.

Placement

A set of instructions may have no more than one space
statement and it need not have one at all.   The space
statement may be placed anywhere in the set.

6.   Specifying a Layout for Printed Items

The next few statement types which we describe are the
various heading statements and the format statements and some

preliminary remarks and definitions are necessary. These
statements specify a sequence of events which takes place in
relation to every item that is selected from the internal
file(s). A single statement may involve several events,
which fall into four categories.

(i) Element-independent events, such as "start a new
     line within the printed item at this point".

(ii) Element extraction and text composition. We can
     copy one or more elements from the item in the
     internal file and build up a piece of text.

(iii) Decoding. Certain coded elements can be converted,
      using a specially constructed code file, before
      being included in the text. We can, for example,
      convert the course code into a descriptive course
      name.

(iv) Formatting the text into a specified field in the
     printed item.

Apart from certain heading statements - the group heading
statements - the order in which the statements appear in the
set of instructions is the order in which they are "obeyed"
when each item is processed, and is therefore important. One
may imagine the computer filling in the fields on the printer
paper working from left to right and downwards, but unable to
backtrack. To illustrate this, let us suppose that we wish
to print each item with its elements laid out in five fields
as follows:

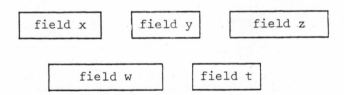

To print them correctly, the fields must be composed,
in the instructions, in the order x,y,z,w,t. The effect
of specifying them in the order y,x,w,t,z would be this:

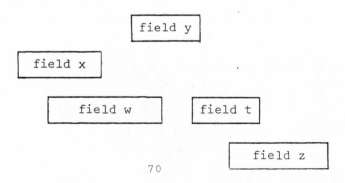

Any element can be extracted from the item and included
in the text to be printed, and the elements are denoted by
their usual tags, for example #201 (order date), #601 (author).
Most elements are printed exactly as they were originally
punched in the external files, but a few elements are printed
in a standard format, regardless of the way in which they
were punched.   The latter are the date elements, #201 and
#202 and the price element, #302.   Dates are printed like
these examples:

                    9/2/70
                    6/10/68
                    23/11/69

Maximum size 8 characters.

     Prices are printed as follows:

Decimal   £125.00   £ s.d.   £11.11.11
           £23.05   £12.1.0
           £5.26   £5.5.2
            50P   10.0

Maximum size 7 characters   Maximum size 9 characters

     If, in the place of an element tag in a print-control
statement, the characters

                    #TODAY

appear, then the date on which the program is executed will be
placed in the text in the same format as elements #201 and #202
as described above.   The same date will be presented for
formatting with each selected item as though it had been
extracted as an element from the item (which, of course, it
will not have been).   This is of use when printing orders
to booksellers, for example.

     It is possible to have some elements decoded before being
printed if a suitable code file is made available to program
PRINT.   The construction of the code file (named SYSCODE) is
explained in Chapter 8.   The elements that can be decoded
are the one-character elements #203 (agent report) and #300
(status), the three-character elements #200 (agent) and #401
to #499 inclusive (courses) and the first character of the
item number (#100).   Decoding is requested by writing the
word DECODED after the element tag in the print-control statement.   For example:

                    #401 DECODED
                    #300 DECODED

     There are four ranges of element tags, and it is possible
to request the inclusion in the printed text of all elements

present in the item with tags in one of the ranges.   We use special tags in the print-control statements as follows:

#400 for the range 401 to 499,
#600 for the range 601 to 699,
#700 for the range 701 to 799,
#800 for the range 801 to 899.

The text will contain all the elements in the specified range, separated by commas. For example, the tag #400 might, for one item, produce

ABX,JEF,JGP

and the tag #600 might produce

YAMEY B.S., HOBART PAPERS. SEE YAMEY B.S., HARRIS R. (ED.) SEE YAMEY B.S.

If there is a null element in the range before the last non-null one, it will be represented in the formatted text by three full stops.   For example,

ABY,...,JEJ

Note that #400 DECODED is not allowed.

We now define a syntactic entity which will be used in describing some of the statements.

element has the following syntax:

num

no DECODED

TODAY

num is either one of the element numbers:

100, 101, 102, 200, 201, 203, 300, 301, 302, 401-499 incl., 500, 601-699 incl., 701-799 incl., 801-899 incl., 900, or one of the four numbers 400, 600, 700, 800, representing the aggregates of elements in one of the four ranges 401-499, 601-699, 701-799 or 801-899.

no is one of the element numbers:

100, 200, 203, 300, 401-499 incl.

The element is used to specify an extraction of data either directly from the item, or indirectly via the decoding mechanism, or from the system (in the case of #TODAY).

The next process to discuss is that of building up text for putting into a field in the printed item. The simplest possibility is to compose a piece of text using a single element. More complicated instructions are often required. We can, for example, build up text by telling the program to extract the author (#601), put 4 spaces after it, extract and add on the title (#701), add 5 spaces and, finally, add all the class numbers (#800). This whole text can then be moved into a field in the printed item. We can involve any element in the composition process and the same element may be used more than once. The user's requirements are communicated to program PRINT using the syntactic unit text in format statements.

text has the syntax:

$$\left.\begin{array}{l} \text{element} \\[1em] (\text{element } \underline{gap} \text{ element . . .)} \end{array}\right\}$$

(i) gap is a number in the range 1 to 120 inclusive. It represents the number of spaces to come between the data extracted by the element's on either side of it.

(ii) The ellipses (. . .) represent as many gap element pairs as are required. The list must end with an element and must have alternating gap's and element's throughout.

Examples of text conclude these preliminary notes.

```
#601
#401 DECODED
(#601,4,#701,5,#800)
(#TODAY,4,#201,2,#200 DECODED)
```

7.   Group Heading Statements

There are two very similar statements in this category.

Prototype A

$$\left.\begin{array}{l} \text{PAGE} \\[1em] \text{P} \end{array}\right\} \quad [\text{start}] \quad \underline{\text{element}} \ ;$$

Prototype B

$$\left.\begin{array}{l} \text{LINE} \\[1em] \text{L} \end{array}\right\} \quad [\text{start}] \quad \underline{\text{element}} \ ;$$

(i) In each case, an abbreviation of the statement keyword to one letter is recognized.

(ii) start is a number between 1 and 120 inclusive.
      Its presence in the statement is optional and
      if it is omitted a value of 1 is assumed. start
      represents a position (or column) on the printer's
      line.

(iii) element has the syntax given on page

Examples

            PAGE 20, #401 DECODED;
            LINE 5 #801;
            P #900;
            P 95, #TODAY;

Function

     The main purpose of the group heading statements is to
extract an element from the items and print it as a heading
for the run of consecutive items which have the same value
for that element.   For example, to print a subject catalogue,
we would firstly sort the file into class number sequence,
using SEQ801 say, and then print it.   We might include in
the set of instructions one such as the second example above:

            LINE 5 #801;

     The class number would then be printed as a heading
only when its value changes as the printing program reads
through the file.

     If a group heading statement is included in the set of
instructions, it is the first to be obeyed for each item
selected for printing.   The data is extracted from the item
and if it is identical to that which was last extracted by
the group heading statement nothing further is done.   Otherwise, if "DECODED" is specified, the decoding is now performed
and the text is formed into a single line for printing.   The
text will begin in position start of the line and anything
beyond position 120 in the line will be lost.

     Two things are now done with this line.

  (i) It is printed immediately (i.e. at the point where
       the element value changes in the file) either at
       the head of a new page if the statement follows
       prototype A ("PAGE"), or simply on a new line with
       one blank line on each side of it if a statement
       like prototype B ("LINE") has been used.

 (ii) The heading line is also saved so that whenever a
       new page is started before the heading changes,
       the line is printed at the top of the page.

If decoding is requested and positions 95 onwards in the heading line are free after the text has been placed in it, the coded element is also placed in the line at position 95.

Placement

No more than one group heading statement can be used in a set of instructions. It can be placed anywhere in the set; it will be the first statement obeyed for each selected item regardless of its position.

8. The Format Statement

We come now to the statement which takes data from items, constructs text and formats it into a specified field on the printer paper.

Prototype

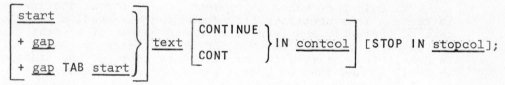

(i)   start is a number between 1 and 120 inclusive. It is a position in a printer line.

(ii) gap is a number between 1 and 120 inclusive. It is a number of spaces on a line.

(iii) If none of the alternatives in the first pair of brackets appear, then the assumption is that the first alternative is present with a value of 1 for start.

(iv) text is as defined in an earlier paragraph (page 73 Its syntax is:

element

(element gap element . . .)

(v)   contcol is a number between 1 and 120 inclusive. It is a position in a printer line. If the CONTINUE-clause is omitted, contcol is assumed to be start if start is given or assumed.

(vi) stopcol is a number greater than both start and contcol, if they are specified, and not greater than 120. It is a position in a printer line. If the STOP-clause is omitted, stopcol is assumed to be 120.

Examples

(a)   5, #601, CONTINUE IN 8, STOP IN 30;

(b)   #102;
     - this is exactly equivalent to
(b)   1, #102, CONT IN 1, STOP IN 120;

(c)   +4 (#601,3,#701,3,#500) STOP IN 95;

(d)   +10, TAB 30, (#701,5,#801);
     - this is equivalent to
(d)   +10, TAB 30, (#701,5,#801) CONTINUE IN 30, STOP IN 120

(e)   4, (#100,1,#300,DECODED), STOP IN 15;
     - this is equivalent to
(e)   4, (#100,1,#300,DECODED), CONT IN 4, STOP IN 15;

Function

     The only part which is present in all format statements
is <u>text</u>.   This specifies, for each item selected, a piece of
text of virtually any length, composed mainly of elements.
See pages 71-73 for a description of how texts are built up.
In describing the function of the other parts of the statement,
we shall assume that we have a piece of text already.

     Firstly, in this explanation a "field" is a rectangular
area on the printer paper containing a particular part of one
or more lines.   A field:

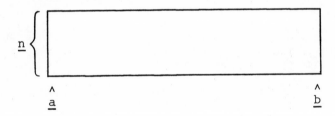

     On the diagram

<u>n</u> is the number of lines in the field and is determined solely
     by the quantity of text put into it.

<u>a</u> is a position on the line, i.e. a column.   It is the first
     column in the field.

<u>b</u> is the last column in the field.

Note that program PRINT assumes that the line is 120 characters
     long, i.e. the page has columns numbered 1 to 120
     inclusive.

When PRINT puts some text into a field and finds that
it is too long for one line, that is it will not fit into
columns a to b in one piece, the program will split it at
spacing or punctuation if that is possible.   We define the
"dynamic end" of the field as the column containing the
rightmost character when the field has been filled.   It is
dynamic because it will vary from item to item, whereas b
is a fixed limit.   In fields of more than one line (n > 1),
the dynamic end may not be the position of the last character
in the first line.

At the other end of the field, a can be a fixed point,
the same for all items, or it can be a floating position
dependent upon previously constructed fields.   a can also
change during the composition of one field in a certain
restricted sense.   We can specify that continuation lines
should start in a different column from the first line of a
field;   one can think of this in terms of moving the left
hand side of the rectangle after the first line has been put
in.

The format statement is designed to enable the user to
specify a and b for one field.   The sequence of format and
other statements in a set of instructions then determines the
layout of the printed item.   The specification of b is
straightforward.   The value of b is the value of stopcol
either as given in the STOP-clause or as assumed if the
STOP-clause is omitted from the statement.

The specification of a depends on the form of the first,
optional, clause in the statement.   There are three possible
ways of setting the value of a.

(i)   start (or clause omitted in which case start is
      assumed to be 1).

      a is set to the value of start.   If that gives
      a column number less than the dynamic end of the
      last field constructed, the whole field will be
      moved down the page to the next free line, other-
      wise the field will be printed to the right of
      the previous field.   If the text requires more
      than one line within the field, continuation
      lines will start in column contcol (remember
      that contcol is assumed to be the same as start
      if it is not specified explicitly).

(ii) + gap

      a is set to the column which is gap clear spaces
      on from the dynamic end of the last field.   So
      a itself is dynamically determined.   Continuation
      lines will be started at a if either the CONTINUE-
      clause is omitted from the statement or the value

of a turns out to be greater than that given for
contcol, otherwise they will start in contcol.

(iii)   + gap **TAB** start

a is set to the column which is gap clear spaces
on from the dynamic end of the last field only if
that is beyond (arithmetically greater than) start,
otherwise a is set to the value of start. This
allows us to tabulate (at start) as much as possible,
but at the same time to guarantee at least gap
spaces between fields. Continuation lines start
at contcol unless a is set to a greater value than
contcol, in which case they start in column a.
When the CONTINUE-clause is omitted, contcol is
assumed to be the same as start.

The reader should try to work out the effects of some of
the examples given above. The art of writing format statements - and, indeed, print-control statements in general - is
quickly learned in a practical situation, and bears a distant
relation to manipulating type for letterpress printing.

Placement

The sequence of format statements and two other types of
statement yet to be described (the heading and skip statements)
determines the relative positions of the fields in each item.
Each of these instructions is obeyed "bearing in mind" what has
preceded it.

9.   Heading Statement

The name of this statement, which must not be confused
with the group heading statements, should not be interpreted
too literally. The product is a line of text at the beginning
of the item or if we so wish at the end or at some point
between.

Prototype

$$\left.\begin{array}{l} \text{HEADING} \\ \text{HEAD} \\ \text{H} \end{array}\right\} \text{[start]}\quad \text{string}\ ;$$

(i)   Two abbreviations of the statement keyword are
recognized.

(ii)   start is a number between 1 and 120 inclusive.
It is a position in a printer line. If it is
omitted, the value 1 is assumed.

(iii) <u>string</u> is any character string of length not
       exceeding 120.   It must be enclosed in quotes
       if it contains any special characters or spaces.

Examples

        HEADING 12, 'DURHAM UNIVERSITY LIBRARY';

        H '   DURHAM UNIVERSITY LIBRARY';

The examples are equivalent to each other.

Function

    The heading statement is obeyed, along with format
statements, for each item selected, in the sequence in which
they occur in the set of instructions.   The <u>string</u> is
printed in each item on a line to itself, starting in
column <u>start</u>, and the line after it is left blank.   If the
heading statement comes before all the format statements,
the <u>string</u> will be the first line of each printed item.
Otherwise, it will occupy the next free line after the
fields that have already been filled in.   The example
above has been used in Durham University, when printing
orders to booksellers, so as to put the source of the order
on each item.

Placement

    The occurrence of a heading statement is optional in
a set of instructions.   There must be no more than one and
it can be placed anywhere in the set.   Its position
relative to format and skip statements is important as
described above.

10.   Skip Statement

Prototype   SKIP ⎫
                         ⎬ [<u>lines</u>] ;
         S   ⎭

 (i) The abbreviation, S, of the keyword is recognized.

(ii) <u>lines</u> is a number between 1 and 29 inclusive.   It
      represents a number of lines in the printed item.
      If <u>lines</u> is omitted from the statement, it is
      assumed to be 1.

Examples   SKIP 2;

              S 3;

              S;   - equivalent to SKIP 1;

Function

Skip statements are obeyed, for each item, in sequence with format statements. The statement means "before constructing the next field, skip to the beginning of the lines'th free line after the fields already filled". The effects will be that (lines-1) lines will be left blank in each item, and that the next field constructed will start at a position in the line which is independent of the previous fields. The first two examples above cause 1 and 2 lines, respectively, to be left blank and the last two examples simply cause the next field to be started on a new line.

Placement

A set of instructions can have several skip statements, or none at all. The number is limited because the PRINT program cannot handle printed items larger than 30 lines, including embedded blank ones. The position of skip statements in the set determines their place in the data formatting sequence.

11.   Execute Statements

There are two types of execute statement, the End statement and the Go statement. They are called "execute" statements because they tell the PRINT program, among other things, to stop interpreting statements and if the set of instructions makes sense, to execute them (i.e. to get on with the actual printing).

Prototype A

         END;

Prototype B

$$\text{GO} \left[\left(\begin{array}{c} \underline{cardfile} \\ \underline{cardfile}\ \underline{column} \end{array} \right\} \right) \right] ;$$

(i)   cardfile is the name of a card file containing print-control statements.

(ii)   column is a number not exceeding 80.   It is a card column number.

(iii) Suppose that the go statement is actually read by PRINT from a card file called this (columns 1 to col). If column is not specified, the value of col is assumed for it, and if cardfile is not specified, this is the assumed card file.

Examples

 (Suppose that the following statements occur, separately, in card file SET, columns 1 to 80.)

(a)   GO (CONTROL,72);

(b)   GO (ALIST);
  - this is equivalent (in this case) to
(b)   GO (ALIST,80);

(c)   GO;
  - this is equivalent to
(c)   GO (SET,80);

 There is, of course, no need to illustrate prototype A, the end statement.

Function

 Both execute statements cause interpretation of the set of instructions to terminate, and printing of the file(s) to start if there are no serious errors in the instructions. They must therefore come at the end of sets of instructions. The other function of the execute statements is to tell PRINT what to do when the lists of items have been printed, and here they differ.

 The end statement is used to terminate execution of program PRINT as invoked by the original PRINT command described in Section 6.1.

 The go statement is used when further printing is required. The PRINT program is to read print-control statements for another listing from card file cardfile, columns 1 to column inclusive. If column is not specified, PRINT should read the statements from the same card columns as it did the last set. If cardfile is not specified or if cardfile is the name of the file from which the go statement was read, the PRINT program will continue reading that file at the beginning of the card immediately following the go statement. If cardfile is CONTROL, the special card file, program PRINT will continue reading it at the card after the last one read from it in the job step. If cardfile is anything else, PRINT will start reading it from the beginning.

 To illustrate the use of the go statement, suppose that we have three card files, ALIST and SET stored on a disk and CONTROL entered with the job on punched cards. We can interpret several sets of instructions from all three files with just one invocation of PRINT. For an example, follow the arrows.

Command: **PRINT CONTROL 72;**

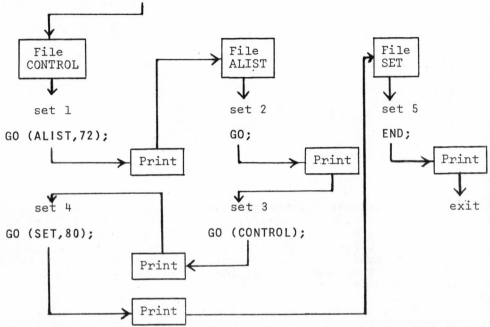

Instruction sets 1 and 4 come from file CONTROL, 2 and 3 from ALIST and 5 from file SET.

Placement

Every set of instructions must have an execute statement at the end of it and that is the only place where an execute statement can occur.

6.3 USE OF PRINT

We illustrate the use of print-control statements with a sequence of examples, all of which print the author, title, date of publication and class number from each item of the file AFILE (which is sorted into author order). Figures 6.1, 6.2 and 6.3 each contain a set of print-control statements and a reproduction of a few items formatted accordingly. Then we give the print-control statements for a catalogue in class number order (figure 6.4) followed by a sample of the output produced by it (figure 6.5).

```
LIST FILE AFILE;
SPACE 1;  /* ALLOW BLANK LINE BETWEEN ITEMS*/
5, #601, CONT IN 7, STOP IN 24;  /*AUTHOR*/
28,#701, CONT IN 30, STOP IN 63;  /*TITLE*/
67,#500, STOP IN 75;  /*DATE*/
80,#801, STOP IN 95;  /*CLASS NUMBER*/
END;
```

ABEL-SMITH B. & TOWNSEND P.	POOR AND THE POOREST	1965	362.50942085
ABRAMS M.H.	MIRROR AND THE LAMP	1953	809.1
ACKLEY G.	MACROECONOMIC THEORY	1962	330.1
ADAM A.	HISTOIRE DE LA LITTERATURE FRANCAISE AU 17E SIECLE.:5V.	1948-56	840.61
ADAM A.	VERLAINE	1967	848.4
ADAMSON L. & DUNHAM H.W.	CLINICAL TREATMENT OF MALE DELINQUENTS	1956	365.937

Figure 6.1   Four tabulated columns

```
LIST FILE AFILE;
SPACE 1;
5,(#601,4,#701,3,#500,5,#801), CONT IN 15, STOP IN 95;
END;
```

ABEL-SMITH B. & TOWNSEND P.   POOR AND THE POOREST   1965   362.50942085

ABRAMS M.H.   MIRROR AND THE LAMP   1953   809.1

ACKLEY G.   MACROECONOMIC THEORY   1962   330.1

ADAM A.   HISTOIRE DE LA LITTERATURE FRANCAISE AU 17E SIECLE. 5V.   1948-56   840.61

ADAM A.   VERLAINE   1967   848.4

ADAMSON L. & DUNHAM H.W.   CLINICAL TREATMENT OF MALE DELINQUENTS   1956   365.937

Figure 6.2   Elements not individually tabulated

```
LIST FILE AFILE;
SPACE 1;
5,#601, CONT IN 7, STOP IN 75;
+4, TAB 22, (#701,3,#500), CONT IN 23, STOP IN 75;
80, #801, STOP IN 95;
END;
```

ABEL-SMITH B. & TOWNSEND P.   POOR AND THE POOREST   1965   362.50942085

ABRAMS M.H.   MIRROR AND THE LAMP   1953   809.1

ACKLEY G.   MACROECONOMIC THEORY   1962   330.1

ADAM A.   HISTOIRE DE LA LITTERATURE FRANCAISE AU 17E SIECLE.   840.61
                     5V. 1948-56

ADAM A.   VERLAINE   1967   848.4

ADAMSON L. & DUNHAM H.W.   CLINICAL TREATMENT OF MALE DELINQUENTS   365.937
                            1956

Figure 6.3   A partially tabulated listing

Figure 6.1 shows a tabulated listing. All the authors are printed in the same field, which starts in column 5, and similarly the titles, dates and class numbers each have their own field, the same for all items. With the indentation of continuation lines in the author field, it is easy to find authors on this list but it suffers from two disadvantages. Firstly, there are large gaps in the printed lines following short elements and one's eye can easily jump to another line while scanning across the page. Secondly, many entries will occupy more than one line and the whole list will be longer than necessary. As in the other examples, the format is restricted to print positions 5 to 95 inclusive so that the list fits the 12" wide folders in use in the library at Durham (a guillotine is applied to the right hand side of the paper). Note also that we start the lines in print position 5 instead of 1. This is to allow room for binding.

One way of overcoming the disadvantages of the fully tabulated format is shown in figure 6.2 Elements are joined into one piece of text before being placed in the field, so the author is the only element tabulated. The disadvantage in this case is the rather unattractive appearance of the whole page. A large indentation of overflow lines is necessary so that one's ability to scan the list for authors' names is not impaired by the intrusion on the left of class numbers and dates.

Figure 6.3 is a compromise. Authors and titles are closer together than in figure 6.1 and in most cases the title is tabulated. Note the position of the overflow line in the last item.

```
LIST FILE CFILE;  /*CLASS CATALOGUE*/
SPACE 1;
L 80,#801;  /*HEADING ON RIGHT TO AID SEARCHING*/
5, #801, STOP IN 79;
+3, TAB 15,#601, CONT IN 16, STOP IN 79;   /*AUTHOR*/
+3, TAB 35,#701, STOP IN 79;               /*TITLE*/
END;
```

Figure 6.4 Print-control statements for a catalogue in class number order. A sample print-out using this set of instructions is displayed in figure 6.5

For further examples of the use of print-control statements, the reader is referred to page 115 in Chapter 7, where a set is given which is intended for a file in course code order and prints the courses as headings (decoded), and to page 145, which contains a set of instructions for printing orders for dispatch to agents.

301

301	SPENCER H.	PRINCIPLES OF SOCIOLOGY ED.ANDRESKI S.
301	STARK W.	FUNDAMENTAL FORMS OF SOCIAL THOUGHT
301	WEBER M.	ECONOMY AND SOCIETY. 3V.
301	WEBER M.	THEORY OF SOCIAL AND ECONOMIC ORGANISATION. EC.T.PARSONS
301	WELFORD A.T. AND OTHERS (EDD.)	SOCIETY. PROBLEMS AND METHODS OF STUDY. REV. ED.
301	WILSON L. & KOLB W.L.	SOCIOLOGICAL ANALYSIS
301	WINCH P.	IDEA OF A SOCIAL SCIENCE
301	WOLFF K.H.(ED.)	GEORG SIMMEL 1858-1918

301.01

301.01	BLACK M. (ED.)	SOCIAL THEORIES OF TALCOTT PARSONS
301.01	COHEN P.S.	MODERN SOCIAL THEORY
301.01	DEMERATH N.J. & PETERSON R.A.(EDD.)	SYSTEM, CHANGE, AND CONFLICT
301.01	GIDDENS A.	POWER IN THE SOCIAL THEORIES OF TALLOTT PARSONS
301.01	GROSS L. (ED.)	SOCIOLOGICAL THEORY. INQUIRIES AND PARADIGMS
301.01	GROSS L. (ED.)	SYMPOSIUM ON SOCIOLOGICAL THEORY
301.01	ISAJIW W.W.	CAUSATION AND FUNCTIONALISM IN SOCIOLOGY
301.01	MACKINNEY J.C. & TIRYAKIN E.A.(EDD)	THEORETICAL SOCIOLOGY
301.01	MANNHEIM K.	IDEOLOGY AND UTOPIA
301.01	MARTINDALE D.	NATURE AND TYPES OF SOCIOLOGICAL THEORY
301.01	MYRDAL G.	VALUE IN SOCIAL THEORY
301.01	PARSONS T.	STRUCTURE OF SOCIAL ACTION. 2V.
301.01	PARSONS T. AND OTHERS (EDD.)	THEORIES OF SOCIETY
301.01	RADCLIFFE-BROWN A.R.	NATURAL SCIENCE OF SOCIETY
301.01	REX J.A.	KEY PROBLEMS OF SOCIOLOGICAL THEORY
301.01	ROSE A.M.	THEORY AND METHOD IN THE SOCIAL SCIENCES
301.01	RUSTIN M.	RECEVANCE OF MILLS SOCIOLOGY
301.01	SOROKIN P.A.	CONTEMPORARY SOCIOLOGICAL THEORIES

301.01

301.01	STEIN M. & VIDICH A.(ED)	SOCIOLOGY ON TRIAL
301.01	TIMASHEFF N.S.	SOCIOLOGICAL THEORY. 3RD ED.

301.04

301.04	BOBBS-MERRILL	BOBBS-MERRILL REPRINTS IN THE SOCIAL SCIENCES (SERIES 'S'-SEE SEPARATE CATALOGUE FOR DETAILS)
301.04	DAHRENDORF R.	ESSAYS IN THE THEORY OF SOCIETY
301.04	HAMMOND P.E.(ED.)	SOCIOLOGISTS AT WORK
301.04	MANNHEIM K.	ESSAYS ON SOCIOLOGY AND SOCIAL PSYCHOLOGY
301.04	MOORE W.E.	ORDER AND CHANGE

Figure 6.5   Sample Printout (using instructions in figure 6.4)

The most frequently used programs in the LFP System have now been described. Here is a list of them:

(i) FINPUT converts an external file (on cards for example) to internal, updating format.

(ii) UPDATE modifies one internal file, using the contents of another.

(iii) FCOPY copies internal files, either in whole or selectively.

(iv) SORT arranges an internal file in a specified order. There is a collection of sequencing routines built into the system.

(v) MERGE interfiles two previously sorted internal files to produce one file.

(vi) CHKSRT checks an internal file to see if it is in a specified order.

(vii) PRINT reads the user's directives from control (card) files and prints formatted lists of items from internal files.

This chapter describes how a librarian uses the commands so as to manipulate files and print lists and catalogues. The information given is mostly specific to the LFP System, but includes some that is just special usage of the operating system (360/OS) and its facilities.

7.1 *PROGRAMS OF COMMANDS*

We can combine the above programs (and some others still to be described) in sequences, thereby achieving considerable flexibility. Users will soon accumulate standard jobs for routine operations.

Let us consider an example and build up a program of commands. The problem is to devise a standard program to update the main file. Program UPDATE works on internal files so the new items, which have been keypunched in the external format, must first be converted to internal format (using FINPUT). We might use the following command:

       FINPUT INDATA 80 ON TEMP BJPX '' ABCDEF ' ';

This reads the external file INDATA (all 80 columns of the cards) and writes the internally formatted items into file TEMP.   The card listing is switched ON so that we shall get a printout of all the cards in INDATA.   Acceptable type-of-publication codes (#102) are B,J,P and X and acceptable status codes (#300) are A,B,C,D,E and F.   Any agent report code (#203) and no #301 codes will be admitted.

UPDATE LBK TEMP LBK OFF;

uses the newly created file TEMP to update the contents of LBK, the main file.   The new version of the file replaces the old.   The last parameter (OFF) allows the program to alter existing items in the file LBK.   UPDATE assumes that LBK and TEMP are in item number (#100) order, but it is tedious to make sure that the new external items are in the correct order, so we insert another command before the UPDATE.

SORT TEMP TEMP SEQ100;

replaces TEMP by itself, sorted into item number order.

We now have the basis for an updating program.   We write a PROGRAM statement at the beginning, to give the program a name, and an END statement at the end, and the program is complete.

```
UPD1 PROGRAM;
     FINPUT INDATA 80 ON TEMP BJPX '' ABCDEF ' ';
     SORT TEMP TEMP SEQ100;
     UPDATE LBK TEMP LBK OFF;
     END;
```

The next thing to do so to prepare data definition (DD) statements for all the files used.   The files mentioned explicitly are INDATA (a card file), TEMP (a new internal file which can be destroyed at the end) and LBK (an existing internal file).   In addition, SORT needs four work files called WORK1, WORK2, WORK3 and WORK4, which would be created especially for the job and destroyed at the end of it. UPDATE will also use WORK1 because it is asked to overwrite the main file (see section 4.2).

When we write DD cards for TEMP and the work files for SORT, we must say how much disk space we need.   We shall assume that LBK already has 3,000 items and that there are 200 items on the cards in INDATA.   In section 4.1 we calcu-lated the requirement for Durham University's items - 45 items per track on a 2314 disk volume.   We should request SPACE=(TRK,(3,1)) for TEMP and (TRK,(2,1)) for the files WORK2, WORK3 and WORK4.   WORK1 must be as large as LBK, (TRK,(66,6)), because it is used by UPDATE.   Disk space allocation will be explained in a later section of this chapter.   At this stage, we have simply applied some of the formulae given in earlier chapters.

Let us estimate the CPU time required for the whole task.

Time = FINPUT time + SORT time   + UPDATE time

   = (approx.) 20 + 0.0021x200x8 + 0.5+0.001x3000
                                +0.05x200
                        + 3 (copy back to LBK)

   = 40 seconds

We now examine the place of the program in an updating routine.   Clearly it cannot be all that is required because there is no provision for safeguarding the main file. Suppose, for example, that LBK is not large enough to take the new information.   That will only be detected while it is being overwritten and we shall have lost the end of the file, which may contain items not included in TEMP (in fact we cannot know exactly what remains in the file without a lot of tedious searching through printouts).   We must be able to recover from such disasters efficiently and one way to ensure that we can is to take a copy of the file at regular intervals on a different disk volume or a magnetic tape.   The following simple program takes a back-up copy of LBK:

```
COPY PROGRAM;
     FCOPY LBK '' BACKUP;
     END;
```

To recover, we run a very similar program (LBK and BACKUP are exchanged) and then do again all the updates that have been done since the last copy was made.

There is another updating procedure which is commonly used in commercial applications of magnetic tape files.   It requires three versions of the main file which are usually referred to as grandfather, father and son.   One updates the son and overwrites the grandfather with the new file; the father is untouched and is thus safe.   If the process is successful, we "rotate" the terminology - the grandfather is now the son, the son becomes the father and the father will be the grandfather in the next updating run.   The following program might be used for this technique.

```
UPD2 PROGRAM;
     FINPUT INDATA 80 ON TEMP BJPX '' ABCDEF ' ';
     SORT TEMP TEMP SEQ100;
     UPDATE SON TEMP GRAND OFF;
     END;
```

The DD statements required are similar to those for UPD1, but we must permute statements for the files SON and GRAND.   Suppose that A, B and C are the names of the data-sets on disk holding the three versions of the file.   The files (SON and GRAND) should be defined as follows:

File Name	Data-set names		
	Jobs 1,4,7,etc.	Jobs 2,5,8,etc.	Jobs 3,6,9,etc.
SON	C	A	B
GRAND	A	B	C

Obviously, an error such as forgetting to change the DD cards between updates can wreak havoc. We must also remember which (of A, B and C) is currently the son so that up-to-date catalogues and lists are produced.

In Durham, the first method is used (programs like UPD1 and COPY). Using the catalogued procedure DLFPMCLG (see Appendix C), the job to run UPD1 consists of 17 cards apart from the cards in INDATA, and we would keep them as a standard job to use over and over again. Even so, there are various modifications which we might wish to make for some runs.

For example, if some of the item numbers (#100) have been changed using element #101, the file LBK may no longer be in order and we shall have to sort the main file. The following command, placed after the UPDATE command, tells us whether LBK is in item number order.

CHKSRT LBK SEQ100;

We can then submit a job to sort the file into item number order if necessary. We could do it all in one job by sorting the file in any case but on a file of 3,000 items about 75 seconds of CPU time would be wasted if it happened to be in order already. It can still be made into a single program by using a conditional statement. Such a statement tests the completion code set by a previously executed command and accordingly continues with or passes over the next command.

It will be recalled that CHKSRT not only prints the result of its check but also communicates it in the completion code. The codes and their meaning are:

(i) 0.   File in sequence

(ii) 4.   File empty (i.e. no items)

(iii) 6.   File not in sequence

(iv) 8 and 12.   Errors

We would wish to sort LBK only if the CHKSRT program
finished with code 6.   The CHKSRT command in the following
modified program is labelled so that it can be referred to.

```
UPD1A PROGRAM;
      FINPUT INDATA 80 ON TEMP BJPX '' ABCDEF ' ';
      SORT TEMP SEQ100;
      UPDATE LBK TEMP LBK OFF;
  CHK CHKSRT LBK SEQ100;
      IF CHK = 6;
      SORT LBK LBK SEQ100;
      END;
```

DD cards are required for the same files as before, but
WORK2, WORK3 and WORK4 must be allocated more space since
they might now be used for the second SORT command.

In the next section we shall deal with the precise rules
for writing commands and assembling them into programs.

7.2   THE LIBRARY FILE PROGRAM GENERATOR

A program of commands such as those appearing in
section 7.1 is the data for the program generator, which
outputs two card files.   These contain the generator's
products, namely:

(i)   A PL/1 program which calls other, previously written
      programs to obey the commands and which handles
      completion code testing, and

(ii) Control statements for the Linkage Editor, which
      specify a program structure to economize on the core
      storage used by the final library file program.

Normally these card files are used in the same job,
being written into temporary data-sets on a disk volume and
removed before the end of the job.   In Durham University a
catalogued procedure (see section 2.4) is used and files are
passed automatically to the PL/1 compiler and linkage editor
programs.   Appendix C contains a copy of the catalogued
procedure (DLFPMCLG) and a brief explanation.

The rest of this section is concerned with the syntax
of commands and other statements and the rules for constructing programs.   The program generator will print messages
describing any errors and warning of possible errors.   It
is necessary to inhibit execution of the later job steps
(PL/1 compilation, linkage editing and execution) if errors
have been detected in the command program, because no PL/1
program would be generated in that case.   The catalogued
procedure DLFPMCLG controls the execution of job steps

according to the outcome of previous steps.

1.   Syntactic Units

As in the print-control language described in Chapter 6, three types of syntactic unit are recognized in the LFP System command language and with the exception of symbols with special meaning, they have the same syntax in the two languages.

(i)   A <u>symbol</u> is either one of the characters

;   =   ¬   <   >

or one of the following pairs of characters (always punched in adjacent card columns)

<=   >=   ¬<   ¬>   ¬=

(ii)   A <u>string</u> is a sequence of characters.   Any character may occur in a <u>string</u>.   Strings are separated from each other by one or more spaces or their equivalent (see iv below).   A <u>symbol</u> need not be separated from a <u>string</u>.   Single quotes (') are used, one at each end, to delimit a <u>string</u> which contains a space (or equivalent) or a <u>symbol</u> or a quote (which would be represented by two adjacent quotes).   The following are <u>string</u>'s:

UPDATE

'#300=DEF' - quotes needed because it contains =

' ' 　　　　 - a blank <u>string</u>

'' 　　　　　 - the empty <u>string</u>

(iii)   A <u>comment</u> is any sequence of characters starting with the pair of characters /* and ending with the character-pair */.   The characters in these pairs must be punched in adjacent card columns. A <u>comment</u> is treated like a space, so it can be used to write comments which are ignored by the program generator.

(iv)   Commas and <u>comment</u>'s are exactly equivalent to spaces and wherever one space may appear, we may write any combination of commas, spaces and <u>comment</u>'s.

2.   Commands

In general, the form of a command is as follows:

[label]   progname   parlist   ;

label is optional (this is indicated by the square brackets
     which are not punched, of course).   It is a name given
     by the user to the command for reference purposes and
     consists of up to 6 letters or digits without embedded
     spaces.   If a command is labelled, label must be
     punched between card columns 2 and 7 inclusive.   No
     two statements in a program may have the same label.

progname is the name of one of the task programs provided
     in the LFP System.   The full list is given in the left
     hand column of figure 7.1.

parlist is a list of strings, called parameters, supplied by
     the user for his particular application.   Each task
     program requires a fixed number of parameters, each of
     a certain type.   They must always be supplied in the
     same order.   Figure 7.1 gives the number of parameters
     required in each command.   The descriptions of the
     programs (Chapters 4,5,6,8 and 9) include explanations
     of the meaning of the parameters.   Syntactically, they
     fall into five categories.   Figure 7.1 contains a list
     of parameter types for each command.

   (i)   File names.   These must be strings of from
         1 to 7 letters or digits, the first of which
         must be a letter.

   (ii) Strings.   Any string is syntactically valid
         for this type of parameter.   The content
         will depend on what is required by the program
         (it might for example be a selection specifi-
         cation).

   (iii) Numbers.   These are strings consisting
         entirely of digits.   They represent whole
         numbers.

   (iv) Switches.   There are two acceptable values -
         ON and OFF.

   (v)   Routine names.   Syntactically, they are
         exactly like file names.   They are the names
         of programs such as the sequencing routines
         listed in figure 5.1.

Note that a command must be terminated with a semicolon.

The whole command, after the optional <u>label</u>, is restricted to columns 8 to 72 (inclusive) of the cards. A command may extend over several cards. Each command must be started on a new card.

Program Name	Number of Parameters	Types of Parameters							
BATCH	4	F	N	Sw	F				
CDLIST	1	F							
CHKSRT	2	F	R						
CODEIN	1	F							
COIND	1	F							
FCOPY	3	F	St	F					
FINPUT	8	F	N	Sw	F	St	St	St	St
FPUNCH	2	F	F						
IMAGE	4	F	N	F	Sw				
MERGE	4	F	F	F	R				
PRINT	2	F	N						
RUNOFF	2	F	N						
SORT	3	F	F	R					
UPDATE	4	F	F	F	Sw				

Key to parameter types:

    F = file name   Sw = switch
   St = string   R = routine name
   N = number

Figure 7.1   Table of LFP System task programs

3.   The Program Statement

Every program of commands must start with a program statement.   The prototype follows:

$$[\underline{label}] \quad \left.\begin{array}{l} \text{PROGRAM} \\ \text{PROG} \end{array}\right\} \quad ;$$

label is an optional name given to the program by the user. The only use that is made of it in the system is that it is printed at the head of the first page of the output from the final program.   The label, if present, consists of up to 6 letters or digits without embedded spaces and must be punched between card colums 2 and 7 inclusive.   It must be a unique name within the program.

PROGRAM and PROG are alternatives, one of which must appear and the statement is concluded with a semicolon.   The statement, after label, is restricted to colums 8 to 72 of the card.

4.   The Conditional Statement

Commands are normally obeyed in the order in which they are written in the program.   However, we might wish to break the sequence at some point depending on conditions arising during execution of the program.   Conditions are detected for this purpose using conditional statements ("if" statements). The conditional statement prototype is as follows:

$$[\underline{label}] \quad IF \quad \left.\begin{array}{l} \underline{label1} \\ \underline{num1} \end{array}\right\} \quad \underline{compare} \quad \left.\begin{array}{l} \underline{label2} \\ \underline{num2} \end{array}\right\} \quad ;$$

label is an optional name given to the statement for reference purposes.   If present, it consists of up to 6 letters or digits with no embedded spaces.   It must be different from the labels of all other statements and commands in the program.   It should be punched between card columns 2 and 7 inclusive.

IF identifies the statement as a conditional one.

label1 and label2 represent labels of commands (i.e. among those named in figure 7.1) in the program.

num1 and num2 represent whole numbers, in other words string's consisting entirely of digits.

Note that label1 and num1 are alternatives and so are label2 and num2.

Note also that label1 (or label2) can be a number

(according to the syntax of labels) and we then have
ambiguity - is the string a case of label1 or of num1? The
following rule solves the problem.   If a string adjacent to
compare is composed entirely of digits, it is regarded as a
value of num1 (or num2) only if no command or other statement in the program has that string as a label.   It is
considered an error if the string is the label of a statement
other than a command.

compare is one of the following symbol's

    =   "equal to"

    ¬   )
) "not equal to"
    ¬=   )

    <   "less than"

    >   "greater than"

    ¬<   "not less than"

    ¬>   "not greater than"

    <=   "less than or equal to" (equivalent to ¬>)

    >=   "greater than or equal to" (equivalent to ¬<)

They all represent comparison relations between two
numbers.

The statement, after the optional label, is restricted
to columns 8 to 72 inclusive of the card.   An "if" statement
must start on a new card.

The two numbers compared in a conditional statement are
as follows:

(i)   If num1 is used, then num1 itself; otherwise the last
      completion code returned by the command named label1
      (if that command has not yet been executed, the code
      is taken to be zero).

(ii) If num2 is used, then num2 itself; otherwise the last
      completion code returned by the command named label2
      (if that command has not yet been executed, the code
      is taken to be zero).

We say the last code returned because it is possible to
have a command executed more than once in one run (though we
rarely have occasion to do that).

An "if" statement must be followed in the program by either a command or another "if" statement or a "goto" statement (the "goto" statement is the next one to be described). The first command or "goto" statement after the conditional statement is called the dependent statement. The conditional statement

IF condition ;

means: "Execute the next statement if and only if the condition is true, otherwise continue with the statement following the dependent statement".

Examples

a) CHECK CHKSRT AMEND SEQ100;
        IF CHECK=6; /*DO SORT IF AMEND IS NOT IN ORDER*/
        SORT AMEND AMEND SEQ100;
        UPDATE LBK AMEND LBK ON;

In this example the conditional statement compares the completion code of the command labelled CHECK with the number 6 and the condition is true if they are equal. The dependent statement is the SORT command. This sequence of statements therefore means: "If file AMEND is not in item number order (SEQ100), sort it into that order. Then update file LBK with AMEND, only allowing new items to be added (switch is ON)".

b)   PROGRAM;
    1 FCOPY LBK '#300=PT' F1;
    2 FCOPY SBK '#300=PT' F2;
    3 MERGE F1 F2 F3 SEQ100;
        IF 1 < 8;
        IF 2 < 8;
        IF 3 = 0;
        PRINT CONTROL 72;
        END;

This is an unnamed program which merges selected parts of two files and then prints a list of items (file CONTROL might contain instructions to print file F3, for example). There are three conditional statements and they all have the same dependent statement, namely the PRINT command. PRINT is executed if and only if all three conditions are found to be true. The condition 1 < 8 in this case means "the completion code of the command labelled 1 is less than the number 8" and not "the number 1 is less than the number 8", because 1 is the label of a command. The meaning of the conditional and dependent statements is "Execute the PRINT program if and only if the two file copies and the merge have worked without error".

5.   The Goto Statement

The statement now to be described causes a break in the normal sequence of execution of commands and directs the computer to resume at another (named) point.   The prototype is:

[label] GOTO   label1   ;

label is an optional name given to the statement by the user.
        If it is present, label consists of from 1 to 6 letters
        or digits (no embedded blanks) punched between card
        columns 2 and 7 inclusive.

GOTO is the statement keyword.   It is simply the words "go"
        and "to" joined together.

label1 is the label of a statement in the program.   It can
        be the name of either a command or an "if" statement or
        another "goto" statement or the end statement.   It may
        not be the label of the program statement (i.e. the name
        of the program).

The statement, after the optional label, is restricted to columns 8 to 72 (inclusive) of the card, and it must start on a new card.

When the statement is encountered during execution of the program, the next statement to be executed is that which has label1 as its label.   "Goto" statements are most frequently used with "if" statements;   there are two common situations.

(i)   Under certain circumstances, we wish to skip past a few
        commands.   A flow-chart representation of this require-
        ment is:

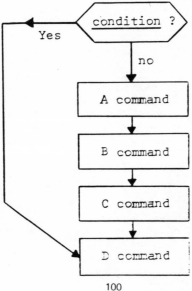

Statements to achieve it would look like this:

```
       IF condition;
       GOTO D;
     A command;
     B command;
     C command;
     D command;
```

(ii) If a certain condition holds, we wish to do one set of commands, otherwise we wish to do another set.

The flowchart:

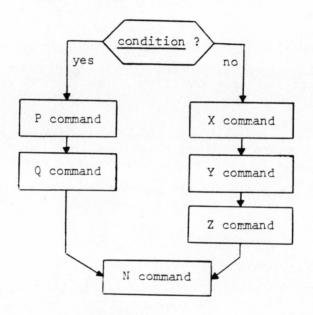

and the statements:

```
       IF condition;
       GOTO P;
     X command;
     Y command;
     Z command;
       GOTO N;
     P command;
     Q command;
     N command;
```

Example

Let us make a temporary amendment to the program called
UPD1 in section 7.1.   We wish to make a backup copy of the
main file (LBK) before we do the updating.   We must not allow
the updating to be done if the copying operation is not
perfectly successful.

```
    UPD1B PROGRAM;
     BKUP FCOPY LBK '' BACKUP;
          IF BKUP¬=0;  /*I.E. IF ANY ERRORS IN FCOPY*/
          GOTO EXIT;   /*    SKIP UPDATING*/
          FINPUT INDATA 80 ON TEMP BJPX '' ABCDEF ' ';
          SORT TEMP TEMP SEQ100;
          UPDATE LBK TEMP LBK OFF;
     EXIT END;
```

6.   The End Statement

The reader has probably already gathered that the end
statement marks the end of the program.   The prototype is:

[label]   END;

label is an optional name given to the statement for reference.
If present, it must consist of from 1 to 6 letters or
digits punched between card columns 2 and 7 inclusive.

END and the semicolon are punched anywhere in columns 8 to
72 inclusive and the statement must start on a new card.

Each program must have exactly one end statement, at the
end of the program.   Its function is to terminate execution.

7.   Programs - Summary and Rules

A program consists of the following three parts:

(i)   A program statement.

(ii)   A combination of commands, "if" statements and "goto"
statements arranged to accomplish the user's task.

(iii)   An end statement.

Commands are executed one after the other in the order
in which they occur in the program, except where that sequence
is disturbed by "if" and "goto" statements.

All commands set completion codes according to conditions
arising during their execution and "if" statements can be used
to test the completion codes of commands which have labels.

The format of LFP System program cards is as follows:

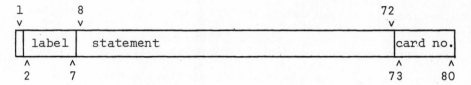

Notes

(i)   The label and the card number are optional.

(ii)   A statement must begin on a new card.

(iii)   A statement may continue onto as many cards as necessary. The label field on continuation cards should be blank.

(iv)   Column 1 of the card has a special use which is not described here. It must normally be blank.

(v)   The remarks made in section 6.2 about noise words in print-control statements are not applicable to the command language.

(vi)   Labels are composed of up to 6 letters or digits with no embedded spaces. No two statements in the same program may have the same label. Labels can be referred to by "if" and "goto" statements as often as the user requires (it is not considered an error if a label is unreferenced).

7.3   *FILES AND DATA-SETS*

Section 2.4 in Chapter 2 introduces the Job Control Language (JCL), which is the user's means of communication with the operating system. In the present section, we concentrate on Data Definition (DD) statements.

All LFP System programs use files of one sort or another. Most files are named by the user in his commands. There are some other files to which programs refer behind the user's back, as it were, using standard file names (for example, the work files, WORK1, etc.). These names, whether invented by the user or not, are merely symbols for channels through which information passes to and from the program. The process of File Definition is that of associating, for the duration of one job-step, a file name to a real data-set on one of the storage media accessible to the computer. The reason for this indirect method in the operating system of

using data-sets is that programs can refer to data in a
device-independent way.   File definition is achieved partly
by information given in the program and partly by DD statements supplied as part of the job.   The LFP System user is
responsible only for providing DD statements containing
information needed to identify the data sets.

This discussion of DD statements is limited to what is
required by the LFP System user and a complete description
is to be found in [1], which is a comprehensive treatment of
the JCL.   Also we omit details of magnetic tape handling
and refer the user to the computer staff, in the first
instance, for that information.

Firstly, we describe the format of DD statements and
the way in which.they are punched into 80-column cards.

The DD Statement

//<u>name</u> DD <u>parameters</u>

The statement starts with the character / in both the
first and second columns of the card.

<u>name</u> is that which connects the DD statement to a file in
the program.   When the catalogued procedure DLFPMCLG
is used, the name of a file in a command is prefixed
by the characters "G." to form <u>name</u>.   There should
be no embedded spaces and <u>name</u> must start in column 3
of the card.

E.g.   //G.LBK
                //G.TEMP

DD must have at least one space on either side of it.   (It
is called the "operation field" of the statement.)

<u>parameters</u> is a list of DD statement parameters, each of
the form

<u>keyword</u> = <u>value</u>

E.g.   UNIT=2314
                DISP=(NEW,KEEP)

Parameters are separated from each other by commas
(the last has no comma after it) and no blanks may
occur in <u>parameters</u> except, as described below, when
the statement will not fit onto one card.   The
parameters can be written in any order in the statement - the <u>keyword</u> identifies the type of information.

Sub-parameters are used when the <u>value</u> consists of

more than one piece of information.   They are
enclosed in parentheses.

E.g.   DISP=(NEW,KEEP)
            DCB=(RECFM=F,LRECL=66,DSORG=DA)

DD statements are punched in columns 1 to 71 (inclusive)
of the cards.   If a statement will not fit onto one card it
can be continued on as many further cards as are necessary.
To continue the parameters field:

(i)   Break the list after the comma following a
       parameter or sub-parameter, before column 72
       (leaving the rest of the card blank).

(ii)   Punch / in both the first and the second
       columns of the next card, leave at least one
       column blank and continue the parameter list
       on or before column 16.

(iii) Continue onto further cards, if necessary, in
       the same way.

We now describe the various parameters which the LFP
System requires us to use.   We shall enumerate the forms
of keyword = value in parameters.

(i)   DSNAME

       The name of a data-set on a disk or magnetic tape.

       E.g.   DSNAME=DUL01LBK
               DSN=DUL01LBK   - DSN is a permitted
               DSN=DCL03XYZ   abbreviation

       This name is recorded on the disk or magnetic tape
       and if a public disk volume is used, there may be
       installation rules governing the choice of name.
       In Durham University, we use names starting with
       the user's job number (e.g. DUL01) followed by
       from 1 to 3 letters or digits.

(ii)   UNIT

       This gives the type of device upon which the data-
       set resides.

       E.g.   UNIT=2314   - IBM 2314 disk storage
                                     facility
               UNIT=(2400,,DEFER) - used for magnetic
                                     tape data-sets

(iii)   VOLUME

The name of the disk volume or magnetic tape upon which the data-set resides or is to be created.

E.g.   VOLUME=SER=UNE040
        VOL=SER=UNE040   - VOL is a recognized
        VOL=SER=DUL01T   abbreviation

(iv)   SPACE

The operating system must know how much space to allocate, on a disk volume, to a new data-set. A 2314 disk volume has 4,000 recording tracks arranged in 200 "cylinders" of 20 tracks each. Space can be requested in units of cylinders or of tracks and an incremental allocation quantity can be given.

E.g.   SPACE=(TRK,10)   - allocate 10 tracks

        SPACE=(CYL,3)   - allocate 3 cylinders
                             (=60 tracks)

        SPACE=(TRK,(20,5)) - allocate 20 tracks
                             initially and
                             increment it by
                             5 tracks at a
                             time as the file
                             grows

        SPACE=(CYL,(2,1)) - allocate 2 cylinders
                             initially and
                             increment by 1
                             cylinder as required

The size of the data-set will be incremented no more than 15 times. If more space is still required, replace the data-set by a new, larger one.

(v)   DISP

This parameter tells the operating system whether the data-set already exists or must be created and what to do with it at the end of the job-step, i.e. whether to keep it or destroy it.

        DISP=(NEW,KEEP)   - create a new data-set,
                             keep it

        DISP=(OLD,KEEP)) - data-set already exists,
        DISP=OLD   )   keep it

        DISP=SHR   - data-set already exists,
                             keep it. Program only
                             reads this data set, so
                             other jobs executing
                             simultaneously may share
                             it.

DISP=(OLD,DELETE) - data-set already exists,
destroy it at the end
of the job-step.

If a DD statement has no DISP parameter, the assumption
is

DISP=(NEW,DELETE)

that is the data-set is created at the beginning
of the job-step and destroyed at the end - it is
a temporary, or work, data-set.

(vi) DCB

This parameter gives information about the organization of the records in the data-set.   It is not
often used in the LFP System because the details are
built into the system's programs.

Writing DD Statements for LFP System Files

We are concerned now with data-sets in disk volumes,
which we categorize firstly into three types: (i) created
in a previous job and extant; (ii) new and to be saved for
later jobs, and (iii) temporary, i.e. new and to be deleted
at the end of the job.

(i) Existing data-sets

The DD cards for these data sets can be written
without regard to the organization of the contents.
The data-set name, UNIT and VOLUME are required to
locate it and the DISP is needed.

Examples

```
//G.LBK DD DSN=DUL01LBK,UNIT=2314,VOL=SER=UNE110,DISP=OLD
//G.SYSCODE DD DSN=DUL01LCO,UNIT=2314,VOL=SER=UNE040,DISP=SHR
//G.SAU DD DSN=DUL01SAU,UNIT=2314,VOL=SER=UNE040,DISP=(OLD,DELETE)
```

(ii) New data-sets (to be saved)

These are data-sets which must be created before
the program can write records into them.   We must
give them a data-set name and specify UNIT, VOLUME,
SPACE and DISP.   Data-sets for internally formatted bibliographic files and for card files (on disk)
can be created with similar DD cards.

Examples

```
//G.SBK DD DSN=DUL01SBK,UNIT=2314,VOL=SER=UNE040,
//      SPACE=(TRK,(40,5)),DISP=(NEW,KEEP)
```

```
//G.CF DD DSN=DUL01CF,UNIT=2314,VOL=SER=UNE110,
//      SPACE=(TRK,(10,2)),DISP=(NEW,KEEP)
```

Note that a data set on disk which is used by the LFP System programs to hold a card file has a capacity of 70 card records per track.

The file of codes used by program PRINT and constructed as described in Chapter 8 is always referred to by the name SYSCODE. The DCB parameter is required when creating a new code file (the catalogued procedure DLFPMCLG supplies this) as follows:

```
DCB=(RECFM=F,LRECL=66,DSORG=DA)
```

(iii) Temporary data sets

These are data-sets needed for files created during a job but not required after the job. Such files are required by some of the programs (e.g. the work files used by SORT) and others are created at the user's discretion (e.g. TEMP, the file of amendments in program UPD1B on page 102). DD cards are constructed in the same way for internal files as for card files on disk. We must specify UNIT, VOLUME and SPACE. No data set name is required and in the absence of the DISP parameter, DISP=(NEW,DELETE) is assumed.

Example

```
//G.WORK2 DD UNIT=2314,VOL=SER=UNE020,SPACE=(TRK,(15,5))
```

Special Types of DD Statement

(i) Files of cards for input

If a card file is to be entered on punched cards, the single DD statement as described above should be replaced by cards such as these:

```
//G.INDATA DD *
```

```
+-----------------------+
|                       |
|      card deck        |
|                       |
+-----------------------+
```

```
/*
```

Note that the program can read file INDATA only once and it may not be used for output. We can include several such files in one job.

(ii)   Files of cards for output

If we wish an output card file to be punched rather than stored on a disk, the DD card to use is (e.g. for file OUTFILE)

//G.OUTFILE DD SYSOUT=B

OUTFILE could be used repeatedly in a program for card output but obviously not at all for input.

(iii)   Dummy files

There is in the catalogued procedure DLFPMCLG the definition of a file called **DUMMY** which has the following properties when used in a program:

As an input, internal file it is empty.

As an output, internal file all items written to it are lost.

As an output, card file all cards written to it are lost.

DUMMY can be used for all of the above in one program, but it cannot be used for input card files. We can introduce an empty card file as follows:

//G.EMPTY DD *
/*

File DUMMY can be used for "dummy runs". This command, for example, checks an external file without actually storing it in internal form:

FINPUT EXTFILE 80 ON DUMMY BJPX '' ABCDEF ' ';

DLFPMCLG - What is provided in the Catalogued Procedure

Four file definitions are provided in the final job-step (step G) of the catalogued procedure DLFPMCLG.

(i)   File DUMMY

(ii)   File SYSPRINT for all the printer output

(iii)   File SYSCODE for decoding elements for printing

(iv)   File WORK1, which is simply a temporary file with an initial size of 5 cylinders (increments by 1 cylinder).   WORK1 can take about 18,000 items in internal format or 28,000 records if used as a

card file.   Note that, although it can be used
by several commands in one program, WORK1 (or any
other file except DUMMY) cannot be used both as
an internal file and as a card file in the same
job.

7.4   *JOB ASSEMBLY*

    A complete LFP System job can now be put together.
We outline the job below and then explain the parts which
have not yet been discussed.

// | JOB card |

// | EXEC card |

//M.SYSIN DD *

             | program of
commands |

/*

//G.etc | DD cards for all the files
used in the program (except
those provided in the catalogued procedure) and any
card decks for input to the
program such as print-
control files and new data
items |

//

    The Library File Program Generator reads the user's
program of commands from its symbolic file SYSIN in the
first job-step (step M) so we must provide a DD statement
with the name M.SYSIN.   The PL/1 compiler and the linkage
editor are executed in job-steps C and L respectively, but
these are not mentioned in the job because the catalogued
procedure defines them completely.

The JOB Card

The JOB card will vary considerably from one installation to another.   The description here is limited to those features of the JOB card which have been commonly used in Durham University for LFP System jobs.

//jobname JOB list,source[,CLASS=x]

// is punched in columns 1 and 2 of the card.

jobname consists of the user's 5-character job number followed by up to 3 letters or digits.   If the user submits more than one job at a time, each should have a distinct jobname.

E.g.   the following can be used by user number DUL01

DUL01ABC
DUL01
DUL01L01

JOB is the operation field of the job statement.   It must have at least one space on each side of it.

list is constructed as follows:

In its simplest form: (date,room)

where date is a 4-figure number and room is from 1 to 4 letters or digits.

E.g.   (0010,C105)   - might be used for a
                                       job submitted in
                                       October (month 10)

If more than 1,000 lines are to be printed, or if any cards are to be punched by the job, list is extended:

E.g.   (0010,C105,,3)   - allow 3,000 lines and
                                       zero cards

            (0010,C104,,,200)   - allow 1,000 lines and
                                       200 cards

            (0010,C105,,4,1000)   - allow 4,000 lines and
                                       1,000 cards

source is a string of no more than 20 letters, digits and full stops; spaces are not permitted.   It identifies the originator of the job.

E.g.   LIBRARY
            R.N.ODDY

111

,CLASS=x is enclosed in brackets (which are not punched
     on the JOB card) because it is not required for every
     job.   x represents a single letter and is called the
     job-class.   It specifies which partitions of core
     storage are suitable for the job and is therefore an
     indication of the amount of core storage used by the
     job.   The job-classes of LFP System jobs submitted
     in Durham University are A (partition size about
     88,000 bytes) and C (partition size about 130,000
     bytes).   Larger ones are available but have not been
     required for any LFP System jobs submitted so far.
     It is not possible to give a simple rule which deter-
     mines core storage requirements for a particular job.
     The first three steps of the job always fit into the
     smaller partition.

If the job-class is not given on the JOB card, A is
     assumed.

E.g.   ,CLASS=C

Sample JOB cards

//DUL01T10 JOB (0003,L17),LIBRARY

//DUL01X JOB (0011,C105,,5),LIBRARY,CLASS=C

//DUL01ABC JOB (0001,LIB,,4,300),T.JONES,CLASS=A

The EXEC Card

The EXEC card required to invoke the catalogued
procedure is as follows:

//[stepname] EXEC DLFPMCLG[,TIME.G=(min,sec)]

stepname is an optional name consisting of up to 8 letters
     or digits.   If present, it must start in column 3 of
     the card and may contain no spaces.

EXEC is the statement's operation field.   It must have at
     least one space on each side of it.

DLFPMCLG is the name of the catalogued procedure.

,TIME.G=(min,sec) is an optional field specifying a CPU
     time allowance for the final job-step (step G) if it
     is estimated that it will require more than 1 minute.
     min is a number of minutes and sec is a number of
     seconds.

Examples

>   //   EXEC DLFPMCLG
>
>   //STEPA EXEC DLFPMCLG,TIME.G=(3,0)

The HOLD Card

When a job's demands on various of the computer's resources exceed certain limits set by the installation management, the job must be held in the input queue until the operator can release it (see section 2.1 and in particular figure 2.3). To hold a job the user places a HOLD card immediately after the JOB card. The format of the HOLD card is as follows (it is not, strictly speaking, a part of the job control language):

>   /*HOLD   message

/*HOLD is punched in columns 1 to 6 inclusive and columns
       7 and 8 are left blank.

message is any brief, clear message to the operator to
       tell him why the job is being held. Card columns
       9 to 80 inclusive can be used. It must include
       the job-class, even if it is A.

Examples

>   /*HOLD   * * 15M ** 5000L ** CLASS=C **

- for a job requiring 15 minutes of CPU time and
    5,000 lines printed.

>   /*HOLD   ** DISK DUL01A ** CLASS=A **

- for a short job requiring access to the private
    disk volume DUL01A.

7.5   *SAMPLE JOBS*

A.   A Course/Author Catalogue.   Job DUL01EXA.

The first sample job is to produce a catalogue of material arranged in order of course code (#401) and, within each course, in author order (#601). The full course name is to be printed as a heading at the top of each page and a new page should be started for each new course. The listing is to include, for each item, the type of publication, the author and title. Only items in stock are to be printed (i.e. omit items unreceived, withdrawn and so on).

The data-set containing the bibliographic file is called
DUL01LBK and it is stored on the public disk volume UNE040.
There are approximately 3,000 items on the file in item number
order.   Disk volumes UNE020, UNE030, UNE040 and UNE999 can
be assumed available and can be used for temporary data-sets.

1.   The Program

We must first sort the file into course/author order,
and then call upon the PRINT program.

```
CCAT PROGRAM;
     SORT LBK COURSE SEQ467;
     PRINT CONTROL 72;
     END;
```

The main file is referred to by the name LBK and the sorted
file is called COURSE - this will be a temporary file.   File
CONTROL is a card file containing print-control statements
designed to produce the catalogue.

2.   The Data-Sets

File LBK is to be read from data-set DUL01LBK on disk
volume UNE040.   The program will not change its contents so
it can be shared with other jobs.

File COURSE is a temporary file.   Assuming that it will
be 10% larger than LBK, due to additional entries, the space
requirement will be (TRK,(73,7)).

Files WORK1, WORK2, WORK3 and WORK4 are required by SORT.
They are temporary files and should each be given
SPACE=(TRK,(55,6)).   WORK1 is defined in the catalogued
procedure with adequate space.

File CONTROL will be included on cards with the job
(note that statements must be confined to columns 1 to 72
inclusive).

File SYSCODE is required for decoding the courses, but
we do not need to supply a DD card because a suitable one is
in the catalogued procedure.

3.   Other Requirements

   (i)   Printed Output
         If we make the simple assumptions that 90% of the
         items in the file are in stock and that 20% of the
         items in. the catalogue will be 2-line entries, the
         catalogue will contain the following number of
         lines:

$$3300 \times \frac{90}{100} \times \frac{120}{100}$$

         = 3564 (plus a few for the headings).

Messages from the system and listings of the
program and print-control statements will take
about 150 lines, so our estimated total printout is rather less than 4,000 lines long.
Depending upon our confidence in the estimate,
we should increase the allowance from the
standard 1,000 lines to either 4,000 or 5,000
lines.   In either case, the job will have to
be held.

(ii)   Core Storage

Any program involving PRINT must have the job-
class C.

(iii)   CPU Time

Total CPU time = SORT CPU time + PRINT CPU time
    = (approx.) 0.0044x3300x12 + 33 seconds
    = (approx.) 210 seconds (= $3\frac{1}{2}$ minutes)

We must use the TIME parameter on the EXEC card.

Note.   In practice, with experience, one is able
to make good estimates very quickly without
doing a great deal of arithmetic.

4.   The Job

```
//DUL01EXA JOB (0004,C105,,5),LIBRARY,CLASS=C
/*HOLD  *** 5000 LINES *** CLASS=C ***
//    EXEC DLFPMCLG,TIME.G=(4,0)
//M.SYSIN DD *
 CCAT  PROGRAM;
       SORT LBK COURSE SEQ467;
       PRINT CONTROL 72;
       END;
/*
//G.WORK2 DD UNIT=2314,VOL=SER=UNE020,SPACE=(TRK,(55,6))
//G.WORK3 DD UNIT=2314,VOL=SER=UNE030,SPACE=(TRK,(55,6))
//G.WORK4 DD UNIT=2314,VOL=SER=UNE040,SPACE=(TRK,(55,6))
//G.COURSE DD UNIT=2314,VOL=SER=UNE999,SPACE=(TRK,(73,7))
//G.LBK DD DSN=DUL01LBK,UNIT=2314,VOL=SER=UNE040,DISP=SHR
//G.CONTROL DD *
  LIST FILE COURSE;
  SELECT ITEMS IF '#300=BDEFMTX';  /*ITEMS IN STOCK*/
  SPACE 1;
  PAGE 20, #401 DECODED; /*COURSE NAMES AS HEADINGS*/
  (#102 /*TYPE*/ 5,#601 /*AUTHOR*/), CONT IN 9, STOP IN 95;
  +4, TAB 30, #701 /*TITLE*/, CONT IN 32, STOP IN 95;
  END;
/*
//
```

B.   A Back-up Copy.   Job DUL01EXB.

    This example is one of the simplest jobs one can submit. We are to create a new data-set holding an exact copy of the file in data-set DUL02SBK on disk volume UNE040.   The copy is also to be called DUL02SBK but is to reside on public volume UNE110.   There are approximately 2,100 items on the existing file.

1.   The Program

```
COPY PROG;
      FCOPY SBK1 '' SBK2;
      END;
```

SBK1 represents the old file and SBK2 the new.   No selection will take place.

2.   The Data-Sets

    File SBK1 is to be read from data-set DUL02SBK on disk volume UNE040.   It can be shared.

    File SBK2 is to be stored in a new data-set on disk volume UNE110 called DUL02SBK.   The data-set is to be kept at the end of the job.   We must specify a SPACE parameter. At 45 items per track we need (TRK,(46,4)).

3.   Other Requirements

  (i)   Printed Output

      Messages and program listing are all that will be produced, so 1,000 lines is ample.

  (ii)   Core Storage

      FCOPY, run on its own, fits well within the small partition, so we shall use job-class A.

(iii)   CPU Time

      FCOPY CPU time = (approx.) 2100/700 = 3 seconds, which is well below 1 minute.

      This is a straightforward short job.

4.   The Job

```
//DUL01EXB JOB (0003,C105),LIBRARY
//    EXEC DLFPMCLG
//M.SYSIN DD *
 COPY PROG;
     FCOPY SBK1 '' SBK2;
     END;
/*
//G.SBK1 DD DSN=DUL02SBK,UNIT=2314,VOL=SER=UNE040,DISP=SHR
//G.SBK2 DD DSN=DUL02SBK,UNIT=2314,VOL=SER=UNE110,
//    SPACE=(TRK,(46,4)),DISP=(NEW,KEEP)
//
```

C.   An Updating Job.   Job DUL01EXC.

     In this final example, we use the updating program
UPD1 from section 7.1 to update the file in data-set DUL01LBK
on disk volume UNE040.   The main file has about 3,000 items
and is in item number order.   New and amendment items will
be contained on cards in the external format and the aim is
to construct a job which can be used many times without any
alteration apart from insertion of the external file.

1.·   The Program

```
     UPD1 PROGRAM;·
          FINPUT INDATA 80 ON TEMP BJFX '' ABCDEF ' ';
          SORT TEMP TEMP SEQ100;
          UPDATE LBK TEMP LBK OFF;
          END;
```

We refer to the main file as LBK.   File INDATA will contain
the external file and TEMP is the temporary internal equivalent to it.

2.   The Data-Sets

     File INDATA will be included with the job on punched
cards.

     File TEMP is a temporary internal file.   Space is
allocated, initially, for about 1,100 items.

     File LBK is to be taken from the data-set called
DUL01LBK on disk volume UNE040.   This file will be overwritten and it cannot, therefore, be used by other jobs at
the same time.

     Files WORK1, WORK2, WORK3 and WORK4 are required by
SORT, and a SPACE parameter compatible with that of TEMP is
SPACE=(TRK,(18,2)).   However, WORK1 is also required by
UPDATE in this program and for that purpose the data-set
must be of similar size to DUL01LBK, i.e. about 70 tracks.
The definition of WORK1 in the catalogued procedure will be
adequate.

3.   Other Requirements

The job given below should be suitable for an updating file of up to about 1,000 items. Printed output and CPU time allowances have been chosen in such a way that the same job will be suitable for any updating file smaller than 1,000 items and a main file of about 3,000 items. Of course, the main file might increase in size significantly if a large file of new items is entered.

(i)   Printed Output

The bulk of the output is produced by FINPUT as it prints a copy of the cards in INDATA. 3,000 lines are allowed.

(ii) Core Storage

UPDATE is quite a large program. We use job-class C on the first run and might be able to use A on subsequent jobs when we know how much core storage it has used.

(iii) CPU Time

A CPU time allowance of 3 minutes will be sufficient to process 1,000 external items.

4.   The Job

```
//DUL01EXC JOB (0005,C105,,3),LIBRARY,CLASS=C
//SA    EXEC DLFPMCLG,TIME.G=(3,0)
//M.SYSIN DD *
 UPD1   PROGRAM;
        FINPUT INDATA 80 ON TEMP BJPX '' ABCDEF ' ';
        SORT TEMP TEMP SEQ100;
        UPDATE LBK TEMP LBK OFF;
        END;
/*
//G.WORK2 DD UNIT=2314,VOL=SER=UNE020,SPACE=(TRK,(18,2))
//G.WORK3 DD UNIT=2314,VOL=SER=UNE030,SPACE=(TRK,(18,2))
//G.WORK4 DD UNIT=2314,VOL=SER=UNE040,SPACE=(TRK,(18,2))
//G.TEMP DD UNIT=2314,VOL=SER=UNE999,SPACE=(TRK,(25,2))
//G.LBK DD DSN=DUL01LBK,VOL=SER=UNE040,UNIT=2314,DISP=OLD
//G.INDATA DD *
#100 D2594£ #300 V£ #401 JER£ #500 1969£ #601 MARTIN D.£
#701 RELIGIOUS AND THE SECULAR  #801 201.7£ *
#100 D2591£ #501 EVOLUTION AND ETHICS(ROMANES LECTURE)£ *
#100 D2573£ #300 E£ *
#100 D2553£ #401 EAF£ *
```

          etcetera

```
/*
//
```

REFERENCE

1   IBM System/360 Operating System: Job Control Language,
    Form C28-6539.
    IBM Corp., Data Processing Division, White Plains, N.Y.

8

In the description of print-control statements in section 6.2 a facility was mentioned for decoding some of the coded elements. By this we mean the replacement in the printout of the code by a descriptive text. The elements which can be decoded during printing are as follows:

(i) The one-character coded elements #203 (agent report) and #300 (status),

(ii) The three-character coded elements #200 (agent) and #401 to #499 inclusive (courses),

(iii) The first character of the item number (#100).

It will be recalled that if the facility is used in a printing job, a special file called SYSCODE is required, which contains information necessary for decoding the elements. This chapter explains how the user constructs a file of code translation data and concludes with the description of a command for obtaining an index of the #400 series codes (courses).

8.1   CODES IN TREES

The user prepares a deck of punched cards giving the codes and their meanings. The program CODEIN reads the card file and constructs a file named SYSCODE on a disk to which PRINT can refer. Before the card file can be punched, the codes must be organized in a "tree" structure and this is often best done diagrammatically. Let us start with the course codes (#401 to #499 range). They are 3-letter codes and Durham University Library is currently using about 200 different codes for undergraduate courses in some 20 departments. As we shall see, the method of preparing the code translation file suggests ways of choosing codes for courses, but for the moment we assume that the codes and their meanings are chosen and that we have a list of them.

The first thing to do is to divide the list into groups according to the first letter of the code. The following list of codes, which is a small one invented for the purpose of this explanation, is so grouped.

group S

    SAA   economics

    SBB   economics - honours (1st year)

    SBC   economics - honours. (2nd year)

    SBD   economics - honours (3rd year)

    SCA   economics - general

    SFA   economics - microeconomics

    SFB   economics - macroeconomics

    SFC   economics - monetary

group T

    TAA   mathematics

    TBA   mathematics - topology

    TCA   mathematics - quantum mechanics

    TFA   mathematics - honours (1st year)

    TFB   mathematics - honours (2nd year)

    TFC   mathematics - honours (3rd year)

    TGA   computing

    TGB   computing - programming

    TGC   computing - compilers

    TGD   computing - business applications

We now draw the root of the tree and the first level of nodes - in this case there are two, one each for the letters S and T.

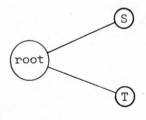

Within each major group (of more than one code) in the list, further subdivisions are made according to the second letter in the code and the next level of nodes are drawn.

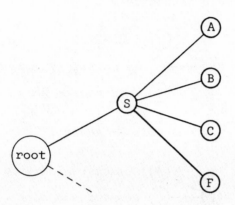

In this half of the tree, there is only one code beginning with SA and similarly with SC, so the nodes labelled A and C are end-points. From the other nodes, we draw another level of nodes corresponding to the third and final letter of the codes. For example:

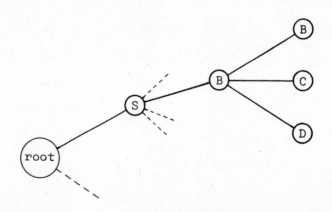

Now we attached the course names to the end-points of the complete tree.

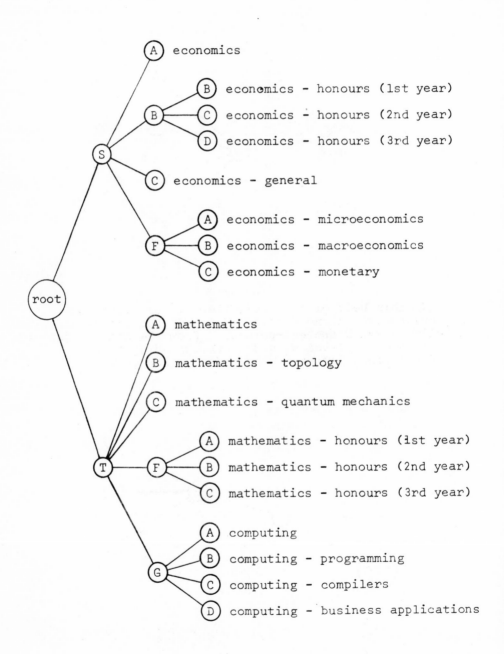

To get the final form of the tree, we move text to the left as far as possible.   The rule is: "if <u>all</u> the nodes connected to the right of a particular node, <u>N</u>, have attached to them text <u>starting</u> with a common string of characters, then move that common part to the left one node - to node <u>N</u>".

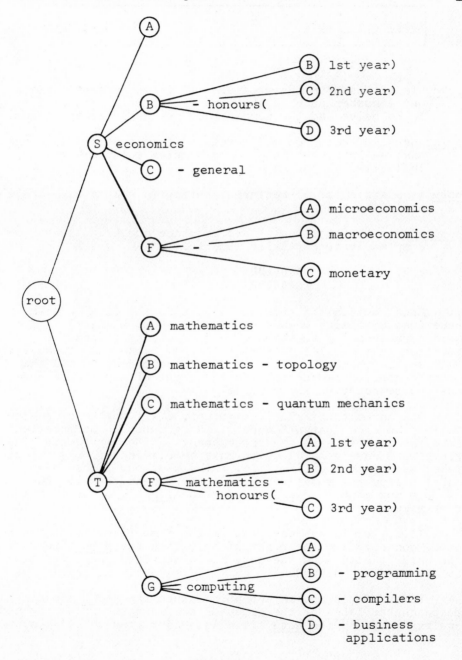

We can now prepare a card file from the code translation
tree. The cards have the following format:

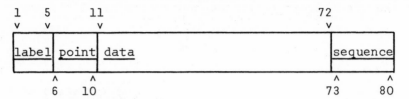

label is not used on every card. If it is present it is a
    whole number punched anywhere within card columns 1 to
    5 inclusive and the number must not be split by spaces.

point does not occur on all cards. It is syntactically the
    same as label but is punched between columns 6 to 10
    inclusive.

data is a string of characters starting in column 11. It is
    explained below.

sequence is the (optional) card sequence number. It can be
    completely or partially numeric.

    e.g.   00000100
                PGC00350

Each node in the tree has a card in the file (we can
sometimes economize when sub-trees are very similar). The
card corresponding to the root node occupies a specific
position in the file; the root of the course code tree, for
example, is the'5th card. Cards corresponding to all the
nodes connected immediately to the right of any single node
must be consecutive in the file.

The cards thus fall into groups, every member of a group
having the same "parent" node. The groups can be inserted
into the card file in any arrangement. The first card of a
group must have a label which must be distinct from every other
label used in the entire file. The user may choose his
label's from the positive whole numbers less than 100,000 and
it does not matter in which order the label's occur in the
card file.

If a node is an end-point in the tree (i.e. if it has no
nodes connected to the right of it), then the point field of
the card is blank and the data field contains the text which
is attached to the node.

If a node is not an end-point, then the point field
contains the label of the group of cards representing the nodes
on its right and the data field is constructed as follows:

(i)   Starting in column 11, the text attached to the
node,

(ii)   Immediately after the text (in column 11 if there
is no text) the character *,

(iii) Starting in the column after the asterisk, in
consecutive columns and terminating in or before
card column 65, the code letters of the nodes
connected immediately to the right in the order
in which they occur in the card group.

The cards for our sample code tree follow:

<u>label</u> <u>point</u> <u>data</u>   <u>sequence</u>

```
          column 11                    column 73
          v                            v
          10*ST                        00000050
                   .                            .
                   .                            .
                   .                            .
10        20ECONOMICS*ABCF             00000230
          30*ABCFG                     00000240
20                                     00000250
          21 - HONOURS(*BCD            00000260
             - GENERAL                 00000270
          22 - *ABC                    00000280
30        MATHEMATICS                  00000290
          MATHEMATICS - TOPOLOGY       00000300
          MATHEMATICS - QUANTUM MECHANICS  00000310
          21MATHEMATICS - HONOURS(*ABC 00000320
          31COMPUTING*ABCD             00000330
21        1ST YEAR)                    00000340
          2ND YEAR)                    00000350
          3RD YEAR)                    00000360
22        MICROECONOMICS               00000370
          MACROECONOMICS               00000380
          MONETARY                     00000390
31                                     00000400
          PROGRAMMING                  00000410
          COMPILERS                    00000420
          BUSINESS APPLICATIONS        00000430
```

To illustrate how the computer uses this file to decode
an element, let us decode course SBD.

(i)   Search the letters after the * on the root card
(00000050) for the 1st letter of the code - S.
It is the 1st letter on the card, so we move on
to the 1st card in the group labelled **10** (card
00000230).

(ii) The text before the * is the first part of the
      translation:

ECONOMICS

Search the letters after the * for the 2nd letter
of the code - B. It is the 2nd in the list, so
we go to the 2nd card in the group labelled **20**
(i.e. to card 00000260).

(iii) Add the text before the * to what we already have:

ECONOMICS - HONOURS(

Search the letters after the * for the 3rd letter
of the code - D. It is the 3rd letter in the
list on the card, so we go to the 3rd card in the
group labelled **21** (i.e. to card 00000360).

(iv) Add the text on the card to produce:

ECONOMICS - HONOURS(3RD YEAR)

There is no * so we have completed the translation.

Notes

(i) The cards 00000340, 00000350 and 00000360 form a
     shared group.

(ii) The economics course codes are allocated more
      economically than the mathematics and computing
      codes. It would have been better to start the
      computing codes with a letter other than T. In
      general, the more text that can be moved to the
      left in the tree, the better, i.e. a hierarchical
      notation, although not essential, is preferable.

(iii) A similar, but usually degenerate, translation
      tree is required for the agent codes (#200) which
      are also three-letter codes.

One-Character Codes

Decoding operates in essentially the same way for
one-character codes but is much more like a straightforward
search.

Example

 The code list for agent reports (#203) might be this:

A expected Jan.-Mar.
B expected Apr.-June
C expected July-Sept.
D expected Oct.-Dec.
E new edition in preparation - no date
R reprinting/binding - no date
N not published
O out of print

 The cards required for the code translation file are:

```
        column 11                              column 73
        v                                      v
    1000*ABCDERNO                              00000030
            .                                      .
            .                                      .
            .                                      .
1000        EXPECTED JAN.-MAR.                 00002330
            EXPECTED APR.-JUNE                 00002340
            EXPECTED JULY-SEPT.                00002350
            EXPECTED OCT.-DEC.                 00002360
            NEW EDITION IN PREPARATION - NO DATE   00002370
            REPRINTING/BINDING - NO DATE      00002380
            NOT PUBLISHED                     00002390
            OUT OF PRINT                      00002400
```

Example

 If we do not wish to use the decoding facility on, say, the first character of the item number, we must nevertheless include a root card (which is blank in the three fields label, point and data:

```
                                      column 73
                                      v
                                      00000010
```

Assembling a Code Translation Card File

 There are five code trees in the file and the root cards must come first as follows:

  Card 1 - root card for #100 (first letter) codes
  Card 2 - root card for #200 codes
  Card 3 - root card for #203 codes
  Card 4 - root card for #300 codes
  Card 5 - root card for #401-#499 codes

 Thereafter, the groups of cards (from all the trees) occur in any order. Special care should be taken over labels.

No two cards in the entire file may have the same <u>label</u>
field and every <u>point</u> field in the file must also be present
as a <u>label</u> field.

Note

It is possible to write a <u>label</u> on a card other than
the first in a group. If it is referred to on another card
(in the <u>point</u> field), then a part of the group starting at
that <u>label</u> is being treated as a group (similar to a general
table in a book classification scheme) in a different part
of the tree.

8.2   *STORING A CODE TRANSLATION FILE*

The card file described in the previous section is not
immediately suitable for use by program PRINT.   (A program
written to decode using the card file would run very
inefficiently.)   The program called CODEIN converts the
card file into the required form.

1.   Command

   <u>label</u> CODEIN <u>cardfile</u> ;

<u>label</u> is optional and is any name by which the command can
      be referred.

CODEIN is the name of the program which converts code
      translation data from its card form in <u>cardfile</u> to an
      internal form suitable for decoding operations.

<u>cardfile</u> is an input card file name.

2.   Function and Notes

The file <u>cardfile</u> contains information necessary for
decoding coded elements and should be prepared according to
the scheme described in section 8.1.   CODEIN reads the card
file called <u>cardfile</u>, performs certain checks upon it and
if it is error-free, writes an equivalent internal form of
it into the file called SYSCODE.   The program produces a
listing of file <u>cardfile</u> and prints descriptive messages if
any errors or suspected errors are detected.   Possible
errors fall into two categories:

 (i) Format and label errors in <u>cardfile</u>, and

 (ii) File definition errors.

There is a limit to the number of labels and label
references that can be managed by CODEIN.   We express it

in terms of the card fields label and point defined in
section 8.1.   Let L be the number of label's and P be the
number of point's used in cardfile.   Then the restriction
is

$$32 \times L + 8 \times P < 16,000$$

Typically, P is approximately $1\frac{1}{4}$ times L and the
number of label's, L, would then be restricted to about
380, which should be sufficient for about 10 times that
number of codes.

The program CODEIN uses a work file called WORK1.

3.   Data Definition Cards

Job control cards are required to define the data-sets
associated with cardfile, SYSCODE and WORK1.

(i)   cardfile is a card file, usually on punched cards
submitted with the job.

(ii)   WORK1 is a normal work file, which has the same
organization as an internal bibliographic file as
far as the operating system is concerned (although
CODEIN does not use it in the same way).   The
space requirement depends on the number of cards
in cardfile, C.   It is, in tracks, the nearest
whole number above the value of C/92.   The catalogued procedure DLFPMCLG provides a suitable
definition for WORK1 with a maximum capacity
corresponding to C=36,800, which is far in excess
of likely requirement.

(iii) SYSCODE is a file with a special organization.
It can be new or extant.   If it is associated
with an existing data-set, the previous contents
are overwritten.   The space requirement depends
on the number of cards in cardfile, C.   Let t be
the nearest whole number above C/43.   Request

$$SPACE=(TRK,t)$$

The file must be stored on a disk volume (or other
direct access device) and not on magnetic tape.
The DCB parameter must be used in the DD statement
for a new data-set as follows:

$$DCB=(RECFM=F,LRECL=66,DSORG=DA)$$

The catalogued procedure DLFPMCLG has the following definition of SYSCODE, which is designed for its use by PRINT:

```
//SYSCODE DD DSN=DUL01LCO,UNIT=2314,VOL=SER=UNE040,
//       DISP=SHR,DCB=(RECFM=F,LRECL=66,DSORG=DA)
```

Note that the DCB parameter is provided, but it will be necessary to override some of the other information when using CODEIN.   Parameters can be overridden individually using a card beginning:

```
//G.SYSCODE DD
```

placed before all the other G-step DD statements in the job.

If the data-set is new, we must code DISP=(NEW,KEEP) and give a space parameter,

E.g.   `//G.SYSCODE DD DISP=(NEW,KEEP),SPACE=(TRK,8)`

If the data-set is extant, we must code DISP=OLD (because the job will change it and it cannot be shared).

E.g.   `//G.SYSCODE DD DISP=OLD`

The user may have more than one code translation file. He will need to change either the data-set name or the volume or both if he wishes to use one not defined in the catalogued procedure.

E.g.   `//G.SYSCODE DD DSN=DUL02ABC,DISP=OLD`

Note that the corresponding change for the benefit of program PRINT, which merely reads the file, is:

```
//G.SYSCODE DD DSN=DUL02ABC
```

4.   Computer Time

CODEIN requires 1 second of central processor time for every 94 cards in cardfile or, expressed another way,

CPU time estimate = 0.0107 x number of cards in cardfile.

5.   Completion Codes

(i)   Completion code 4 if there is a suspected error in cardfile which the user should be warned about. SYSCODE will be written.

(ii)   Completion code 8 if there are errors in <u>cardfile</u>
       or if any of the files are not properly <u>defined</u>.
       SYSCODE will not be successfully written.

(iii) Otherwise, the completion code will be set to 0.

8.3   *PRINTING AN INDEX OF CODES*

     There is a program in the LFP System called COIND which
prints an index of the course codes (#401) used in a particular file with their translations.

1.   Command

     <u>label</u> CO IND <u>intfile</u> ;

<u>label</u> is optional and is any name by which the command
       can be referred.

'CO IND is the name of the program which produces an index
       of the course codes occurring in file <u>intfile</u>.

<u>intfile</u> is an input internal file name.   The file is
       assumed to be in one of the course code orders.

2.   Function and Notes

     COIND reads through file <u>intfile</u> extracting all the
different course codes (#401) <u>used in</u> the file (which is
assumed to be sorted using one of the sequencing routines
SEQ467, SEQ476 or SEQ486).   The program decodes the·
elements using file SYSCODE and prints codes and translations side by side in two columns.   The list of courses
is printed twice; one list is in alphabetical order of
code, and the other is in alphabetical order of course name.

     The file SYSCODE is of the type produced by program
CODEIN (see section 8.2) and is used in the same way as by
PRINT for decoding elements.

     It'is operationally efficient to run COIND when
catalogues or lists in course order are being produced,
because a sorted file will already be available.   For
example, the following command might be placed after the
SORT command in program CCAT of section 7.5:

                COIND COURSE ;

3. Data Definition Cards

Job control cards are required to define data-sets for the files <u>intfile</u> and SYSCODE.

  (i) <u>intfile</u> is an input internal file which has, of course, been previously created.

 (ii) SYSCODE must be defined on a special data-set as created by a previous run of CODEIN (see section 8.2). The catalogued procedure provides a definition for.SYSCODE which is suitable so long as the data-set name and volume are correct.

4. Computer Time

The central processor time required by COIND should not exceed

$$0.002 \times I + 0.0074 \times C \text{ seconds,}$$

where I is the number of items and C is the number of different #401 codes in <u>intfile</u>.

If, for example, we have employed 500 codes in a file of 10,000 items, it will take no more than

$$0.002 \times 10,000 + 0.0074 \times 500 = 23.7 \text{ seconds}$$

of CPU time to execute COIND.

5. Completion Codes

  (i) Completion code 4 if there are no codes (#401) in <u>intfile</u>.

 (ii) Completion code 8 if either <u>intfile</u> or SYSCODE is not properly defined.

(iii) Otherwise, the completion code will be 0.

FILE UTILITY

PROGRAMS

9

In this final chapter, we describe the functions of the five remaining programs in the LFP System. Two of them are designed to work on bibliographic files and the other three do not require their files to have any particular type of content.

(i) FPUNCH reads a bibliographic file in internal format and produces the externally formatted equivalent in a card file.

(ii) BATCH reads an external bibliographic file augmented by certain instructions for generating extra items and produces a new external (card) file, which is suitable for input to program FINPUT.

(iii) IMAGE copies a card file. It can be used to store a card file, such as a control file for PRINT or even a program of commands, on a disk volume. The cards can be numbered by IMAGE or numbers can be removed. The contents of the cards are immaterial.

(iv) CDLIST lists a card file on the printer.

(v) RUNOFF makes copies of printout produced by other jobs. We can store a printout on a disk instead of printing it and then use RUNOFF to copy it to the printer as many times as required.

9.1 FILE CONVERSION (INTERNAL TO EXTERNAL FORMAT)

1. Command

    <u>label</u> FPUNCH <u>intfile</u> <u>extfile</u> ;

<u>label</u> is optional and is any name by which the command can be referred.

FPUNCH is the name of the program which reads an internal file (<u>intfile</u>), converts its items to the external format and writes them into the card file <u>extfile</u>.

<u>intfile</u> is the name of an input internal file.

<u>extfile</u> is the name of an output card file which will contain items in external format.

2.   Function and Notes

FPUNCH reads the internal file <u>intfile</u> item by item
and writes the items, externally formatted, into card file
<u>extfile</u>.   The output card file can be on a disk volume or
a magnetic tape or punched by the computer on cards.   Each
external item starts in column 1 of a new card (or 80-byte
record) and the last eight columns (73-80) are automatically
filled with an 8-digit card number (starting at 00000010
and incrementing by 10).   The program will use as many
cards as are necessary to complete the item.

As regards the distinction between the normal and
updating formats, the equivalence between the internal
and external files is exact.   We illustrate this with an
example.   The original external item as read by FINPUT is:

#100 S0731£ #102 B£ #300 H£ #401 MAX£ #500 1962£
    #601 IVERSON K.E.£ #701 A PROGRAMMING LANGUAGE£ #900 WILEY£ *

If the internal item produced by FINPUT were subjected to
the treatment of program FPUNCH, the external item would
come out unchanged.   If, however, the internal item, which
is in updating format, were first converted by UPDATE into
normal format, then FPUNCH would produce the item:

#100 S0731£ #102 B£ #200 £ #201 £ #202 £ #203 £ #300 H£
#301 £ #302 £ #401 MAX£ #500 1962£ #601 IVERSON K.E.£
#701 A PROGRAMMING LANGUAGE£ #900 WILEY£ *

Note that there is a difference between the represen-
tation of the ranges of elements #401 to #499, #601 to #699,
#701 to #799, #801 to #899 and all the other elements in the
"blank" cases.   The former are "absent" (for economy of
storage) and the latter are null.

The file names <u>intfile</u> and <u>extfile</u> must be different
because they represent different types of file.

3.   Data Definition Cards

Job control cards are required to define the data-sets
associated with <u>intfile</u> and <u>extfile</u>.

(i)   <u>intfile</u> is an input internal file which has been
      created previously.

(ii) <u>extfile</u> is an output card file.   The data-set
      can be an existing one which previously held a
      card file and will now be overwritten, or it can
      be a new one or the card punch.   The card punch
      is used by including a DD card as:

//G.CARDS DD SYSOUT=B

The space requirement for storing a card file on a 2314 disk volume is 1 track for every 70 cards in the file.   The user must therefore estimate the number of cards (80-byte records) which are to be produced and that will depend upon how he has used the elements within the items.   In Durham University, an item as formatted by FPUNCH typically requires 3 cards.   We can discover exactly how many cards will be produced by executing the command:

FPUNCH LBK DUMMY;

The output card file will be lost (DUMMY) and therefore requires no space on a disk, but the program informs us how many cards it has formatted.

4.   Computer Time

The following formula will give an estimate of the central processor time required in terms of the number of items in the file (I) and the number of cards or 80-byte records produced (C).

$$\text{CPU time} = 0.0041 \times I + 0.0126 \times C \text{ seconds}$$

If, for example, the file contains 500 items and there are 3 cards per item in the externally formatted file, then

$$I = 500 \quad \text{and} \quad C = 1,500,$$

so the CPU time is estimated to be

$$0.0041 \times 500 + 0.0126 \times 1500 = 20.95 \text{ seconds.}$$

5.   Completion Codes

(i)   Completion code 8 if the files are not properly defined.

(ii)   Completion code 12 if an item in intfile cannot be read.   This is not usually the fault of the user.

(iii)   Otherwise the completion code will be 0.

9.2   AUGMENTED EXTERNAL FILES

Section 3.4 contains the rules for constructing items for an external file.   We now recapitulate the syntax of a file in external format.

(i)   An element is punched:

<u>tag</u> <u>text</u> £

<u>tag</u> is one of the usual element numbers (see
      figure 3.2).

E.g.   #302

Spaces are allowed between the # and the
number, but not within the number.

<u>text</u> is the value of the element.   Any sequence
      of characters not including #, £ or * is
      allowed.   Spaces at the beginning and end
      of the <u>text</u> will be ignored.

£ is the terminating character.

(ii) An item consists of one or more elements, optionally
      separated by spaces.   The last element is followed
      by a *.   An item may contain no two elements with
      the same <u>tag</u> and it must contain an item number
      (element #100).   The elements may appear in any
      order in the item.

(iii) An item is called a deletion item if, in the
      syntactic position of an element, it contains
      either

DELETE
or DELETE £

(iv) An external file is a sequence of one or more
      items, as defined above, optionally with spaces
      between them.

     This is the form of file read by FINPUT and written by
FPUNCH.   We shall define a type of card file called an
augmented external file by adding to the above syntax, and
it will be suitable for input to program BATCH (see section
9.3) but not to program FINPUT.

     An augmented external file consists of the following
units arranged in any sequence:

(i)   Normal items as occur in an external file.

(ii) Selection statements, which represent groups
      of primitive items, consisting of item numbers
      only.

(iii) "Batch" items, which specify elements common
      to a number of items in the file.

The Selection Statement

    The usual syntax notation is used - brackets ([ ])
enclose optional clauses and alternatives are stacked one
above the other with a brace (}) on their right.   The
prototype selection statement is:

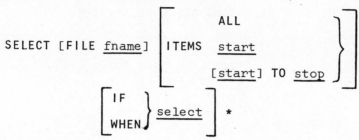

SELECT [FILE fname] ITEMS start / ALL / start / [start] TO stop

[IF / WHEN] select *

fname is the name of an internal file.

start is either an item number or the word FIRST.

stop is either an item number (alphabetically/numerically
    greater than start if that is specified as an item
    number) or the word LAST.

select is a selection specification with the syntax
    described in section 4.4.   select should be enclosed
    in quotes if it contains any of the characters:
    space, comma, #, £, *.

    There are three optional clauses in the statement called
the "file" clause, the "item" clause and the "if" clause.

    If the file clause is omitted, fname is assumed to be
the same as the fname given or assumed in the previous
selection statement in the file.   Note that the first
selection statement in the augmented external file must have
a file clause.

    If the item clause is omitted from the statement, the
default clause

            ITEMS ALL

is assumed.

    In the absence of an explicit if clause,

        IF ' '

is assumed.

Examples

    SELECT FILE LBK IF '#300=A' *

    SELECT ITEMS D1200 TO D1299 *

    SELECT FILE SBK ITEMS D2000 IF '#102=BJ' *

Function of the Selection Statement

    The selection statement stands for a list of items, each
consisting solely of an item number:

                    #100 itemno £ *

    There is one such item corresponding to each item in the
internal file fname which both (a) has an item number in the
range specified in the item·clause and (b) satisfies the selection criterion in the if clause.   itemno is the same as the
#100 element of the corresponding item in fname.   The absence
of the item or if clause implies its irrelevance in choosing
items for inclusion in the list represented by the selection
statement.   (That is what is meant by the default clauses, of
course.)   We must now define how the range of item numbers is
obtained from the item clause.

    Firstly, file fname must be in item number (#100).order.
ITEMS ALL and ITEMS FIRST TO LAST and clauses which imply one
of these mean that the range is from the first item number in
fname to the last.

ITEMS start TO stop.   The range is all the item numbers in
fname from start to stop, inclusive of start and stop if they
are, respectively, in fname.   (It is not an error if either
start or stop is not the number of any item in fname.)

Batch Items

    A batch item is syntactically like a normal item but the
#100 element is replaced by the word

                        BATCH

Examples

    BATCH #300 A£ #200 COM£ *

    BATCH DELETE *

No batch item should have a #100 element.

Function of Batch Items

The whole item, apart from the word BATCH, is to be appended to every normal item (including those implied by selection statements) after this batch item and before the next (if there is one).

The batch item which simply nullifies the effect of the previous one without itself having any effect is:

BATCH *

Examples of Augmented External Files

(i) Assume that the file KBK contains items numbered consecutively starting with D0001. We show first an annotated augmented external file and then the normal external file which it represents.

The augmented file:

```
#100 D0317£ #300 H£ *          - normal item
BATCH #102 J£ *                - application of batch
#100 D0513£ *                                    item
SELECT FILE KBK ITEMS D0732 TO D0735 *
#100 D0915£ #302 2.50£ *
BATCH #102 B£ *               - application of batch
#100 D0916£ *                                    item
SELECT ITEMS D0918 TO D0921 *
```

The normal file:

```
#100 D0317£ #300 H£ *
#100 D0513£ #102 J£ *
#100 D0732£ #102 J£ *
#100 D0733£ #102 J£ *
#100 D0734£ #102 J£ *
#100 D0735£ #102 J£ *
#100 D0915£ #302 2.50£ #102 J£ *
#100 D0916£ #102 B£ *
#100 D0918£ #102 B£ *
#100 D0919£ #102 B£ *
#100 D0920£ #102 B£ *
#100 D0921£ #102 B£ *
```

(ii) Suppose that the status (#300) H means "withdrawn" The following augmented external file can be used to generate an updating file to remove the records of withdrawn material from the file SBK:

```
BATCH DELETE *
SELECT FILE SBK IF '#300=H' *
```

9.3   *THE BATCH PROGRAM*

The LFP System program called BATCH will read a file in augmented external format (see previous section) and expand it into the normal external file which it represents - a file suitable for input to the program FINPUT (section 4.1).

1.   Command

   label BATCH augfile column switch extfile ;

label is optional and is any name by which the command
      can be referred.

BATCH is the name of the program which reads a card file
      (augfile) in augmented external format and writes
      the file (extfile) in normal external format.

augfile is the name of an input card file containing an
      augmented external file.

column · is a number not exceeding 80.   It specifies the
      last column from which data is to be taken (e.g. 80
      if the whole card in augfile is read, 72 if columns
      73-80 are ignored as in the case of numbered cards).

switch is either ON, if a printed copy of the card file
      augfile is required, or OFF if the printout is to be
      suppressed.

extfile is the name of an output card file which will
      contain items in external format.

2.   Function and Notes

Program BATCH reads the card file augfile containing augmented external items and applies the batch items and selection statements to produce a file in normal external format, which it writes into the card file extfile.   The syntax and meaning of batch items and selection statements are given in section 9.2.   The items are written to extfile in the same format as program FPUNCH uses.   Each item starts in column 1 of a new card (or 80-byte record) and columns 73 to 80 inclusive are used for a card number (starting at 00000010 and incrementing by 10).

Items in augfile do not receive the full checking that FINPUT gives them, but the syntax is checked and messages are printed to indicate errors and warn of possible errors. If an error is detected in a normal item, that item is skipped and processing continues with the next one.   If, however, an error is found in a batch item, the run is terminated immediately because such errors would propagate through the file.

The file names augfile and extfile must be different.
The normal way to define them is to make augfile a deck of
cards in the job and extfile a temporary file on a disk
volume which is read by program FINPUT straightaway.   Note
that if augfile contains no batch items or selection statements (i.e. it is an ordinary external file), the items in
extfile will be identical to those in augfile.

3.   Data Definition Cards

Job control cards are required to define the data-sets
associated with augfile, extfile and any internal files
mentioned in the file clauses of selection statements in
augfile.

(i)   augfile is an input card file which can be on punched
cards submitted with the job or in a previously
created data-set on a disk volume or magnetic tape.

(ii)   extfile is an output card file.   The data-set can
be a previously created one, in which case it is
overwritten, or it can be a new one, or it can be
punched onto cards.   Space must be allocated if it
is a disk data-set (70 cards per track).

(iii)   The internal files from which item numbers are
extracted must be data-sets created previous to
the execution of the BATCH command.

4.   Computer Time

The central processor time required by BATCH can be
estimated from the following formula:

$$0.04 \times C_I + 0.0078 \times C_O + 0.0014 \times I \text{ seconds}$$

where C_I = number of cards (or 80-byte records) read from
augfile

C_O = number of cards (or 80-byte records) written into
extfile

I = number of items read from internal files referred
to in SELECT's

5.   Completion Codes

(i)   Completion code 4 is set in cases of syntax error
when either corrective action can be taken or a
normal item can be ignored.

(ii)   Completion code 8 is set if either card file is
not properly defined, in which case the execution
is terminated, or a batch item is found to be in
error (execution is terminated), or various syntax
and file definition errors occur in a selection
statement, in which case the statement is ignored.

143

(iii) Completion code 12 is set if there is a format
error in an internal file mentioned in a selection
statement.   This is not usually the fault of the
user.   Processing proceeds with the next item
after the selection statement, but the contents of
extfile will be most unreliable.

 (iv) Otherwise, the completion code is set to 0.

6.   Example - An Ordering Program

     The LFP System has no facilities for accounting and
therefore it is not currently feasible to use it for full
scale ordering.   However, orders can be printed automatically
to be sent to the agents and this example shows how it is
done.   We assume that these two status codes (#300) are
used in the main file LBK:

          A   meaning "to be ordered"

          C   meaning "on order"

LBK is assumed to be in item number (#100) order.   We
require a program which will print an order for each item
in LBK with the status A and then change the status to C.
We do not wish to make out items by hand for the updating
process.

     We shall have to make estimates based on the size of
LBK and the number of items to be ordered.   Let file LBK
contain 3,000 items.   Estimates will allow for up to 250
items with status A.

The Program

```
ORDER PROGRAM;
        FCOPY LBK '#300=A' TEMP /* TEMP CONTAINS THE
                ITEMS TO BE ORDERED */;
        BATCH SYSIN 80 ON AMEND /* SYSIN REFERS TO TEMP,
                WHICH IS STILL IN ITEM NUMBER ORDER */;
        SORT TEMP TEMP SEQ200 /* AGENT/PUBLISHER ORDER */;
   OUT  PRINT CONTROL 72;
        IF OUT>4;
        GOTO EXIT; /* SKIP UPDATE IF PRINT NO GOOD */
        FINPUT AMEND 72 /* RECORDS ARE NUMBERED */ ON TEMP
                /* CAN USE TEMP AGAIN NOW */,' ',' ',C,' ';
        UPDATE LBK TEMP LBK OFF;
   EXIT END;
```

We define file SYSIN as follows:

```
//G.SYSIN DD *
   BATCH #300 C£ #201 7/12/70£ *
   SELECT FILE TEMP *
/*
```

TEMP is a temporary file which will contain at most 250 full items, so allocate it SPACE=(TRK,(5,1)).

AMEND is a temporary file to take at most 250 cards (one for each short amendment item); we allocate it SPACE=(TRK(4,1)).

The other files which require definition are LBK, WORK1 (for SORT and UPDATE), WORK2, WORK3 and WORK4 (for SORT), CONTROL (defined below) and SYSCODE.

```
//G.CONTROL DD *
  LIST FILE TEMP; /*PRINT ORDERS*/
  SPACE 5;
  PAGE 6,#200 DECODED; /*AGENT*/
  H 10,'DURHAM UNIVERSITY LIBRARY';
  12,(#100,19,#TODAY);
  17,#601,CONT IN 19,STOP IN 66; /*AUTHOR*/
  SKIP;
  21,#701,CONT IN 23,STOP IN 66; /*TITLE*/
  21,(#900,2,#500),CONT IN 23,STOP IN 66; /*PUBLISHER,DATE*/
  72,#302; /*PRICE*/
  END;
/*
```

The reader may wish to work out what the orders will look like, and how many lines of output to expect for 250 orders.

An estimate for the CPU time required for 250 orders can be made:

$$
\begin{aligned}
\text{CPU time} =\ &\text{FCOPY CPU time} + \text{BATCH CPU time} \\
&(\qquad 6 \qquad +\qquad 2.4 \qquad) \\[4pt]
&+ \text{SORT CPU time} + \text{PRINT CPU time} \\
&(0.005 \times 250 \times 8 \quad +\qquad 5 \qquad) \\[4pt]
&+ \text{FINPUT CPU time} + \text{UPDATE CPU time} \\
&(\qquad 15 \qquad + 0.5 + 0.001 \times 3000 + 0.05 \times 250) \\[4pt]
=\ &(\text{approx.})\ 55\ \text{seconds.}
\end{aligned}
$$

The job-class will certainly have to be C.

9.4   *COPYING CARD FILES*

1.   Command

    label **IMAGE** <u>infile</u> <u>column</u> <u>outfile</u> <u>switch</u> ;

<u>label</u> is optional and is any name by which the command can be referred.

145

IMAGE is the name of the LFP System program which copies the data from one card file (infile) to another (outfile).

infile is an input card file name.

column is a number not exceeding 80. Characters are copied from columns 1 to column of file infile.

outfile is an output card file name.

switch is either ON or OFF. If it is ON, columns 73 to 80 inclusive are used for card sequence numbers and the data from infile is placed in columns 1 to 72 of the cards in outfile. If switch is OFF, all 80 columns of the cards in outfile are used. This parameter can be used independently of column.

2. Function and Notes

. Program IMAGE copies the characters from the field, determined by column, of the cards (or 80-byte records) in infile to the cards in outfile, using either 80 or 72 card columns. All the characters in columns 1 to column of the input cards (or records) will be written into the output records and there is not necessarily a one to one correspondence of cards in the two files.

The file names infile and outfile must be different.

The effects of four commonly used combinations of parameters are given below.

(i)   IMAGE INPUT 80 OUTPUT OFF;

This command produces in OUTPUT an exact copy of the cards in INPUT.

(ii) IMAGE INPUT 80 OUTPUT ON;

All the characters in INPUT are written in groups of 72 to OUTPUT and the output cards are numbered. There will be 11% more cards in OUTPUT than in INPUT.

(iii) IMAGE INPUT 72 OUTPUT OFF;

This is the reverse process of the previous example. The last eight columns of the cards in INPUT are eliminated in the copy. There will be 10% fewer cards in OUTPUT than in INPUT.

(iv) IMAGE INPUT 72 OUTPUT ON;

File OUTPUT will contain numbered cards containing

exact copies of columns 1 to 72 of the cards
in INPUT.   We can use this command to number
cards (or records) when we know that columns
73 to 80 are free.

The IMAGE program can be used to manipulate external
files - to store them on disk or to number them - and it
provides a simple way to store programs of commands and
print-control statements on a disk so that reference can
be made to them by other jobs.

3.   Data Definition Cards

Job control cards are required to define the data-sets
associated with files <u>infile</u> and <u>outfile</u>.

(i)   infile is an input card file and should either be
held in a previously created data-set on a disk
volume or magnetic tape or be submitted with the
job on cards.

(ii)   <u>outfile</u> is an output card file.   This can be
<u>punched</u> onto real cards or be stored in a data-set
on a disk volume, for instance.   The space
requirement is, as usual, 1 track for every 70
card records.   The data-set can be either a new
one or an extant one in which case the previous
contents are overwritten.

4.   Computer Time

To obtain an estimate of the CPU time required by IMAGE,

(i)   allow 1 second for every 1,000 cards in <u>infile</u>,

(ii)   if the number of cards in <u>outfile</u> will differ
from that in <u>infile</u>, increase the time by 10%.

(iii) if <u>switch</u> is ON, i.e. the records in <u>outfile</u>
are to be numbered, double the time allowance.

E.g.   If file INPUT contains 10,000 card records, the
command

IMAGE INPUT 80 OUTPUT ON;

should be allowed

(10 + 10% of 10) x 2 seconds

i.e. 22 seconds

5.   Completion Codes

  (i) Completion code 8 is set if either file is not properly defined.   No copying will be done.

(ii) Otherwise, the completion code will be 0.

6.   Example - Using Stored Programs

    We give two jobs in this example. The first uses IMAGE to store a program of commands and a print-control file, and the second uses the two stored card files.   At the end of section 9.3 the major constituents of a job to print orders were given and it is clearly a rather complicated job.

    The following job (DUL01E6A) stores the program called ORDER and the print-control statements in two separate data-sets on a disk volume.   Comments have been removed for compactness.   The stored versions are numbered.

```
//DUL01E6A JOB (0003,C105),LIBRARY
//        EXEC DLFPMCLG
//M.SYSIN DD *
 STORE    PROGRAM;
          IMAGE IN1 72 PROGF ON /*STORE PROGRAM*/;
          IMAGE IN2 72 PRINTF ON /*STORE PRINT-CONTROL
                                  STATEMENTS*/;
          END;
/*
//G.PROGF DD DSN=DUL01ORP,UNIT=2314,VOL=SER=UNE040,
//        DISP=(NEW,KEEP),SPACE=(TRK,1)
//G.PRINTF DD DSN=DUL01ORQ,UNIT=2314,VOL=SER=UNE040,
//        DISP=(NEW,KEEP),SPACE=(TRK,1)
//G.IN1 DD *
 ORDER    PROG;
          FCOPY LBK '#300=A' TEMP;
          BATCH SYSIN 80 ON AMEND;
          SORT TEMP TEMP SEQ200;
    OUT   PRINT CONTROL 72;
          IF·OUT>4;
          GOTO EXIT;
          FINPUT AMEND 72 ON TEMP,' ',' ',C,' ';
          UPDATE LBK TEMP LBK OFF;
    EXIT  END;
/*
//G.IN2 DD *
  LIST FILE TEMP; SPACE 5; P 6,#200 DECODED;
  H 10,'DURHAM UNIVERSITY LIBRARY';
  12,(#100,19,#TODAY);
  17,#601,CONT IN 19,STOP IN 66;
  S; 21,#701,CONT IN 23, STOP IN 66;
  21,(#900,2,#500),CONT IN 23,STOP IN 66; 72,#302;
  END;
/*
//
```

Now we can use the files in our jobs to produce orders.

```
//DUL01E6B JOB (0012,C105,,2),LIBRARY,CLASS=C
//      EXEC DLFPMCLG,TIME.G=(3,0)
//M.SYSIN DD DSN=DUL01ORP,UNIT=2314,VOL=SER=UNE040,DISP=SHR
//G.WORK2 DD UNIT=2314,VOL=SER=UNE020,SPACE=(TRK,(5,1))
//G.WORK3 DD UNIT=2314,VOL=SER=UNE030,SPACE=(TRK,(5,1))
//G.WORK4 DD UNIT=2314,VOL=SER=UNE040,SPACE=(TRK,(5,1))
//G.TEMP  DD UNIT=2314,VOL=SER=UNE999,SPACE=(TRK,(5,1))
//G.AMEND DD UNIT=2314,VOL=SER=UNE999,SPACE=(TRK,(4,1))
//G.LBK DD DSN=DUL01LBK,UNIT=2314,VOL=SER=UNE040,DISP=OLD
//G.CONTROL DD DSN=DUL01ORQ,UNIT=2314,VOL=SER=UNE040,DISP=OLD
//G.SYSIN DD *
    BATCH #300 C£ #201 7/12/70£ *
    SELECT FILE TEMP *
/*
//
```

Note

     Data-sets DUL01ORP and DUL01ORQ contain 10 and 7 card
records respectively.   They have each been allocated the
smallest possible space - 1 track - and even that is far too
large, since it has a capacity of 70 cards.   If it is
required to store many very small card files (of the order
of 10 cards per file) a "library" data-set can be created on
a disk volume with the partitioned organization which enables
files to occupy less than a track and yet not waste the
remainder.   IMAGE can be used to add new members to this
library.   The computer staff should be consulted when such a
library is required.

9.5   *PRINTING CARD FILES*

1.   Command

     <u>label</u> **CDLIST** <u>cardfile</u>

<u>label</u> is optional and is any name by which the command can be
     referred.

CDLIST is the name of the program which prints out the contents
     of the card file <u>cardfile</u>.

<u>cardfile</u> is an input card file name.

2.   Function

     CDLIST reads the cards (or 80-byte records) in the card
file <u>cardfile</u> and prints out their contents, one card per line.

3. Data Definition Card

A job control card is required for the input card file
cardfile. It is either a previously created data-set on a
disk volume or magnetic tape or a deck of cards contained
in the job.

4. Computer Time

The central processor time required by CDLIST is
approximately 2 seconds for every 1,000 cards (records) in
cardfile.

5. Completion Codes

(i) Completion code 4 is never set by CDLIST.

(ii) Completion code 8 is set if cardfile is not
properly defined. No list will be produced.

(iii) Otherwise, the completion code will be 0.

9.6 *STORING PRINTOUTS*

This section is not, as might be thought from the title,
concerned with the storage in the library of the vast piles
of paper obtained from the computer's printer over the months.
It is concerned with a method of saving processor time in the
production of more than one copy of a printout.

All printing that is done by the LFP System programs is
achieved by sending line-records to a file called SYSPRINT,
which is normally associated with the printer by a DD card in
the catalogued procedure DLFPMCLG. Now, instead of printing
this file, we can store it on a disk and then, in a subsequent
job, run off copies of the file on the printer.

Notes

(i) If we wish to store a printout on a disk volume
(or magnetic tape), we must store all the output
from the final step of the job (step G). None
of it will be printed at the time.

(ii) Each copy of the output produced from a previously
stored printer file will be the complete job-step
printout of the program that stored it.

We show how to store a printer file through an example.

```
//DUL01E96 JOB (0010,C105),LIBRARY,CLASS=C
//      EXEC DLFPMCLG,TIME.G=(5,0)
//M.SYSIN DD *
```

```
        ┌─────────────────────────────────────────┐
        │ program of commands (to produce         │
        │ an author catalogue, for example)       │
        └─────────────────────────────────────────┘
```

```
/*
//G.SYSPRINT DD DSN=DUL01PRT,UNIT=2314,VOL=SER=UNE040,
//          DISP=(NEW,KEEP),SPACE=(TRK,(60,5)),
//          DCB=(RECFM=VBA,LRECL=125,BLKSIZE=1254)
//G.WORK2  ┌──────────────────────────────────────┐
          │ DD  . . .                             │
          │                                       │
          │ etcetera                              │
          └──────────────────────────────────────┘
//
```

The DD statement beginning //G.SYSPRINT overrides the statement in the catalogued procedure. With the suggested DCB parameter, a track on the disk will hold at least 50 lines (full 120 character records). If, for example, it is known that the average length of the lines will be 90 characters, the track capacity will increase to 65 lines.

The LFP System program RUNOFF will read a printer file (referred to by a name other than SYSPRINT) and copy it to file SYSPRINT as many times as required. It should be remembered that there are other ways of producing multiple copies of printout.

(i)   Use printer stationery with carbon paper (see operations staff).

(ii) Request more than one copy of the whole job's output (see operations staff).

(iii) Run the job more than once.

A combination of methods may be advantageous for large printing tasks. If, for example, we have to produce 30 copies of an author catalogue, each 4,000 lines long, we might print the list 10 times using triple forms. 40,000 lines would still be considered a very large printing job on a university machine (see section 2.1) and the operational staff might prefer that the job be divided into two of 20,000 lines. The method would therefore be to submit three jobs:

(i)   Produce formatted author catalogue in a printer file on a disk volume.

151

(ii)   Print 5 copies on triple forms using program
       RUNOFF.

(iii) Print 5 copies on triple forms using program
       RUNOFF and delete the stored printer file.

Program RUNOFF

1.   Command

     <u>label</u> **RUNOFF** <u>pfile</u> <u>copies</u> ;

<u>label</u> is optional and is any name by which the command can
        be referred.

RUNOFF is the name of the program which produces copies
        for the printer of the printout stored in <u>pfile</u>.

<u>pfile</u> is the name of an input file containing properly
        formatted lines for printing.   It must be different
        from SYSPRINT.

<u>copies</u> is any positive whole number.

2.   Function

     RUNOFF copies the line-records in <u>pfile</u> to the standard
printer file, SYSPRINT, <u>copies</u> times.   The beginning and
end of each copy are marked START and END.

3.   Data Definition Card

     A job control statement is required to define file
<u>pfile</u>, which should be contained in a previously created
data-set on a disk or magnetic tape.   The data-set should
have originally been written via the file SYSPRINT in a
previous job.

4.   Computer Time

     The central processor time required by RUNOFF is
approximately 1 second for every 500 lines printed.   Expressed
another way, that is

     0.002 x number of line records in <u>pfile</u> x number of
                                                  copies printed

5.   Completion Codes

  (i)   Completion code 4 is never set by program RUNOFF.

  (ii) Completion code 8 is set if file <u>pfile</u> is not
        properly defined.

  (iii) Otherwise, the completion code will be 0.

The organization of internally formatted bibliographic
records, created and manipulated by LFP System programs, is
shown in figure A.1.   The diagram contains eight strips which
are to be imagined joined together.   It shows the positions
of the various elements in the item.   The numbers just above
the strips are byte (character) numbers in the record and those
below the strips give the lengths of the elements in bytes.
Some of the information is stored in character form, which
means that each character in the element (including spaces)
is represented by a code occupying one byte of storage.   There
is also some numerical information which is stored in binary
(a number occupies either one or two bytes of storage).   In
a normal file (as opposed to an updating file) the fields are
used as follows:

Name	Length	Description
RId	1	Record identifier. This is always the character 0.
Item Number	5	Element #100 (characters).
TPC	1	Type of publication code, #102 (character).
Agent	3	Element #200 (characters).
Order Date	6	Element #201. Characters, ddmmyy.
Date Received	6	Element #202. Characters, ddmmyy.
ARC	1	Agent report code, #203 (character).
STC	1	Status code, #300 (character).
SPC	1	(Spare, #301).
Price	6	Element #302. Characters, either llssdd or Dlllpp
ALP	2	Author list pointer (range #601 to #699). Position, in binary, of NA field. If there are no author elements, ALP=0.
TLP	2	Title list pointer (range #701 to #799). Position, in binary, of NT field. If there are no title elements, TLP=0.

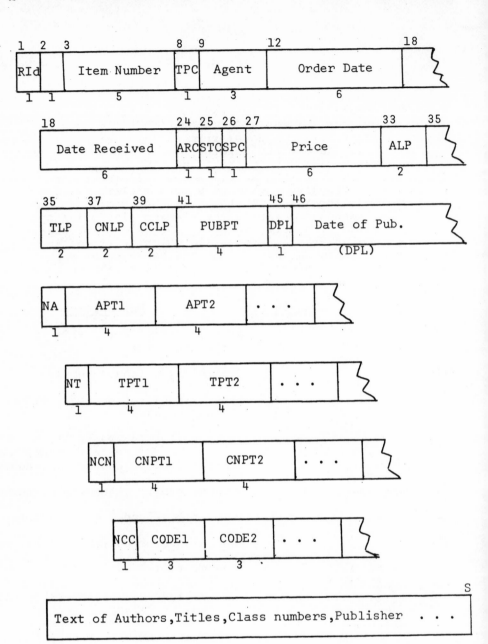

Figure A.1   The internal format for bibliographic
records.   Record size, S, is restricted
to 2470 bytes.

Name	Length	Description
CNLP	2	Class number list pointer (range #801 to #899). Position, in binary, of NCN field. If there are no class number elements, CNLP=0.
CCLP	2	Course code list pointer (range #401 to #499). Position, in binary, of NCC field. If there are no course code elements, CCLP=0.
PUBPT	4	Publisher pointer (#900). Position and length, in binary, of text of publisher. If there is no publisher, PUBPT=0.
DPL	1	Date of publication length of text (#500), in binary. If there is no date, DPL=0.

* * * Fields below here are of variable length and/or position * * *

Name	Length	Description
Date of Pub.	DPL	Date of publication text (#500). If present, this always starts in position 46.
NA	1	Number (in binary) of author elements (#601, etc.). This is followed immediately by NA 4-byte fields, APT1, etc. If ALP=0, fields NA, APT1, etc. are omitted from the item.
APT1	4	Author pointer 1 (#601). Position and length, in binary, of the text of the author. If #601 is null and there exists a later element in the range, APT1=0.
APT2	4	Author pointer 2 (#602). See APT1. An item can have up to 100 APTn fields.
NT, TPT1, TPT2, etc.		As NA, APT1, APT2, etc., but for titles (range #701 to #799).
NCN, CNPT1, CNPT2, etc.		As NA, APT1, APT2, etc., but for class numbers (range #801 to #899).

Name	Length	Description
NCC	1	Number (in binary) of course code elements (#401, etc.). This is followed immediately by NCC 3-byte fields, CODE1, etc. If CCLP=0, fields NCC, CODE1, etc. are omitted from the item.
CODE1	3	Course code 1 (#401). The code in character form.
CODE2	3	Course code 2 (#402). The code in character form. An item can have up to 100 CODEn fields.
Text		All the textual information referred to in the pointer fields described above.

The Updating Format

In items created in the updating format by program FINPUT, the absence of elements is indicated as follows:

Element	Field concerned	Contents of field
#100	Item Number	Never absent
#102	TPC	)
#200	Agent	)
#201	Order Date	)
#202	Date Received	) The first byte of the field contains the character #
#203	ARC	)
#300	STC	)
#301	SPC	)
#302	Price	)
#401-#499		See note (i) below
#500	DPL	The character #
#601-#699		)
#701-#799		) See note (ii) below
#801-#899		)
#900	PUBPT	The character # in the first byte

Notes on the Updating Format

(i)   If all course codes (#401-#499) are absent from the
      item, field CCLP contains zero in binary. If there
      are course codes, and there is a gap in the element
      numbers present, the CODEn field corresponding to
      the absent element has # in the first byte.

(ii) If all the authors (#601-#699) are absent, field ALP
      is zero. If there are authors, and there is a gap
      in the element numbers, the APTn field corresponding
      to the absent element has the character # in the
      first byte.

      Similarly for titles (#701-#799) and class numbers
      (#801-#899).

(iii) If a replacement item number (#101) is present, the
      6-character field shown in figure A.2 is inserted
      immediately after the Date of Pub. field (or, if
      that is absent, the DPL field).

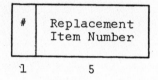

#	Replacement Item Number

 1   5

Figure A.2   The internal form of element #101

(iv) A deletion item has the format given in figure A.3.
      The RId field (record identifier) is the character R
      for a deletion item.

1 2 3

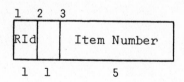

RId		Item Number

 1   1   5

Figure A.3   The internal format for a deletion
             item.   RId is always R for deletion
             items.

This appendix contains, as samples, instructions used in Durham University for:

(i) (Library instructions)   Completion of updating forms (abridged).

(ii) (Computer Unit instructions)   Key-punching details from the forms onto 80-column cards to produce external files.

Most of the detail is local, conventional application of the general rules given in Chapter 3.   Figure B.1 illustrates two completed forms and figure B.2 shows how the items might be punched in an external file.

B.1   *COMPLETION OF FORMS*

General notes

(i) Alphabetical characters are written in capitals.

(ii) Write clearly.   Use the following convention:

letter O   numeral Ø

It should be clear where blanks (spaces) are intended: use the symbol Ƅ if the occurrence of the space is not obvious or if more spaces than one are required in consecutive positions.

(iii) The characters # and * may not be written in any box on the form.   £ may be used for one purpose only (see iv).   Prices should never be written with the £ sign.

(iv) The updating form is used both to add new items to the files and to alter items already there. When writing a form for a new item, enter information in the appropriate boxes.   Any combination of boxes (but always including the item no.) may be used.   To amend an existing item, fill in the "Item no." box and enter the altered or new details in the appropriate boxes.   Whatever is written in the box completely replaces any previous element in that position.   To remove an element from the stored item, enter £ in the box.

#100 Item no. **DØ544**		LIBRARY COMPUTER FILE UPDATING FORM	Delete (tick)	Continuation no.
#102 Type	#200 Agent **COM**	#201 Order date **13/8/68**	#202 Receipt date **12/9/68**	
#300 Status **E**	#302 Price **2.5Ø**	#500 Pub date **1956**	#801 Class **192.9**	
#401 Course **DDM**	#402 **DPR**	#403	#404	#405	#406

#601 Author

LEWIS H.D.(ED.)

#701 Title **CONTEMPORARY BRITISH PHILOSOPHY SERIES 3. 2ND ED.**

#900 Publisher

ALLEN & UNWIN

Continued (tick)

#100 Item no. **D1641**		LIBRARY COMPUTER FILE UPDATING FORM	Delete (tick)	Continuation no.
#102 Type ǂ	#200 Agent	#201 Order date	#202 Receipt date	
#300 Status **F**	#302 Price	#500 Pub date **1964**	#801 Class	
#401 Course	#402 **MAF**	#403	#404	#405	#406

#601 Author **#6Ø2 DEVIZES MUSEUM (SHELVED AT ANNABLE)**

#701 Title

#900 Publisher

Continued (tick)

Figure B.1. Items on Updating Forms. A new item (top) and a typical amendment to an existing item.

```
#100 D0544£ #200 COM£ #201 13/8/68£ #202 12/9/68£ #300 E£ #302 2.50£ #500 1956£
#801 192.9£ #401 DDM£ #402 DPR£ #601 LEWIS H.D.(ED.)£ #701 CONTEMPORARY BRITISH
PHILOSOPHY SERIES 3. 2ND ED.£ #900 ALLEN & UNWIN£ *

#100 D1641£ #102 £ #300 F£ #500 1964£ #402 MAF£ #602 DEVIZES MUSEUM (SHELVED AT
ANNABLE)£ *
```

```
                                                                    column 73
                                                                       v
#100 D0544£ #200 COM£ #201 13/8/68£ #202 12/9/68£ #300 E£ #302 2.50£ #500000002180
0 1956£ #801 192.9£ #401 DDM£ #402 DPR£ #601 LEWIS H.D.(ED.)£ #701 CONTE00002190
MPORARY BRITISH PHILOSOPHY SERIES 3. 2ND ED.£ #900 ALLEN & UNWIN£ * 00002200

#100 D1641£ #102 £ #300 F£ #500 1964£ #402 MAF£ #602 DEVIZES MUSEUM (SHE00031770
LVED AT ANNABLE)£ * 00031780
```

Figure B.2   Externally formatted items.
Two ways of punching the items in figure B.1,
firstly without and then with card numbering
in columns 73 - 80.

(v) To have an item deleted from a file, enter the
item number only and tick the "Delete" box.
The item will no longer exist on the file and
will not, therefore, appear on printouts. A
dated manual record of deletions should be kept.

(vi) Details can be continued on one or more further
files if there are more elements in a range than
are allowed for on the form, e.g. more than one
author or more than six courses. Tick the
"Continued" box on the original updating form,
number subsequent forms 1, 2, etc. in the
"Continuation no." box, and repeat the item no.
each time. Elements (such as long titles)
should not be split between forms, but if
necessary a special note to the punch operator
attached.

Notes about the boxes

(vii) #1ØØ Item no.

Every completed form, including continuation
forms, must bear an item number 5 characters
long. In Durham, "numbers" consist of a letter
and 4 digits, e.g. D1931. This is the record
identification for updating processes; it is
essential to enter the correct item numbers for
amendments and deletions and of course to avoid
duplicating numbers. In order that an item
should appear in catalogues and lists, it must
exist in a file and have an "item no.". There
may be items without exactly corresponding books.

(viii) #1Ø2 Type

A single letter, selected from the code list,
indicating the type of publication.

J means that the item is a periodical article,
M means that it is a Bobbs-Merrill reprint.

Leave the box blank for all other items.

(ix) #2ØØ Agent

A three-letter code indicating the supplier of
the book (consult code list).

(x) #2Ø1 Order date and #2Ø2 Receipt date

Use the form 29/11/69

(xi)   #300 Status

A one-letter code chosen from the following list:

A   to be ordered

B   to be ordered (copy transferred from main
       collection meanwhile)

C   on order

D   on order (copy transferred)

E   received

F   transferred copy, not ordered (including
       books borrowed from elsewhere)

G   cancelled order (no transfer available)

H   withdrawn after receipt

J   withdrawn transfer

M   transferred for Michaelmas term only

P   transferred for Epiphany term only

R   transferred for Easter term only

T   transferred for Michaelmas and Epiphany
       terms only

V   transferred for Epiphany and Easter
       terms only

X   transferred for Easter and Michaelmas
       terms only

Note.   Statuses M, P, R, etc. are for books for
which demand is cyclic and the copy is moved into
and out of the collection.   The item remains in
the files all the time but only appears in catalogues when the book is "in".   Statuses G - J
allow records to be kept of unsuccessful orders
etc., and of books put into limbo when demand
evaporates.

(xii)   #302 Price

Use the form pounds.pence, e.g. 2.50

(there must be two numbers, so 50p is written
0.50).

(xiii) #401 Course, #402, etc.

Enter three-letter codes, from the code list, for
the course(s) for which the item is recommended.
If more than 6 codes are required, alter the

numerical tags and use continuation forms as
necessary.   For example:

~~#401~~ Course	~~#402~~	#403
#407 JDA	#408 £	

When a file is sorted for printing a course
catalogue, additional entries are generated
so that an item will appear in as many places
as it has course codes.

(xiv)   #500 Publication date

Enter year of publication of this edition.

(xv)   #601 Author

Surname first, then initials (no commas).   If
the 'author' is an editor, (ED) follows.   Two
authors' names are separated by &.   If there
are more than two, the first is given, followed
by **AND OTHERS**.   (Note that & files before A)
For works of joint editorship, add **(EDD)** to the
end of the element.

Examples

        LIPSET S.M.
        LIPSET S.M. & BENDIX R.
        LIPSET S.M. AND OTHERS
        LUARD E.(ED)
        MORGAN T. AND OTHERS(EDD)

Official publications are entered under the
issuing body, e.g. DEPARTMENT OF ECONOMIC
AFFAIRS.

(xvi)   Further author entries, #602, #603, etc.

The following comments also apply to additional
titles (#702,#703, etc.) and class numbers
(#802,#803, etc.).   When a file is sorted into
author order, an extra item will be generated
and filed for each additional author, tagged
#602, etc., and these will be printed as added
entries.

```
┌─────────────────────┬──────────────────────────────┐
│ #601 Author         │ #602 DEPARTMENT OF           │
│                     │     EDUCATION - CENTRAL      │
│ PLOWDEN B.          │ ADVISORY COUNCIL             │
│                     │ (SHELVED AT PLOWDEN)         │
└─────────────────────┴──────────────────────────────┘
```

Material is shelved according to the main
author (#601), so reference to it is included
in added author entries.

To add another author entry, or when using a
continuation form:

```
┌─────────────────────┬──────────────────────────────┐
│ #601 Author         │ #602   GEWIRTH A.            │
│                     │      (SHELVED AT MARSILIUS)  │
│                     │                              │
└─────────────────────┴──────────────────────────────┘
```

To remove the 2nd author:

```
┌─────────────────────┬──────────────────────────────┐
│ #601 Author         │ #602  ƶ                      │
│                     │                              │
│                     │                              │
└─────────────────────┴──────────────────────────────┘
```

(xvii)   #701 Title

The sorting programs determine the order of the
items by straightforward character comparisons;
space comes first, followed by punctuation, then
the letters in alphabetical order and lastly the
numerals 0-9 (see Chapter 3, figure 3.1). Delete
articles, prepositions and other non-significant
words from the beginning of titles, and be sparing
and consistent in the use of punctuation and
quotation marks.   Edition, volumes and editor
(where different from the author) are given at
the end of the title, e.g.

6TH ED.   3V   VOL 2   ED. J.SMITH

Additional titles (#702, etc.) are permissible in
the same way as authors (see xvi).

165

(xviii) #8Ø1 Class

       Dewey number. Additional class numbers
       (#8Ø2, etc.) are allowed (see xvi).

  (xix) #9ØØ Publisher

       This box is used for three purposes. If a
       book is to be ordered, enter the publisher,
       and SBN. If the item is a periodical article
       (xerox copy, etc.) enter journal reference
       prefixed by 7, e.g.

          7 BR.J SOCIOL. 12 PP 9-17

       Alternatively, if there is important informa-
       tion concerning the item, which cannot be
       accommodated in the record, use the Publisher
       box for notes, prefixed by 9, e.g.

       9 CONSULT MANUAL RECORD FOR STATUS

  (xx) Send the completed forms to the computer data
      preparation service with any general instruc-
      tions, concerning card numbering for instance,
      attached.

B.2 KEYPUNCHING FROM FORMS

Note

    In Durham University, the average speed of key-punching
has been found to be 10,000 keystrokes per hour, working
directly from forms such as those in figure B.1.

General punching instructions

    An item is all the data written on one or more forms.
Normally, it will all be on one form, but if the "Continued"
box is ticked, expect to find a number in the "Continuation
no." box on the next form. In the latter case, the Item
goes on to include all forms up to and including the first
one without the "Continued" box ticked.

    Work through each Item looking for boxes to the right
of the numbers which have something written in them. For
each of these boxes, type the number followed by one space,
the contents of the box, the £ symbol (unless the box itself
contains a £ already) and another space.

e.g.

#201 Order date	#202 Receipt date
7/3/70	£

would be punched

#201 7/3/70£ #202 £

Note.　If a continuation form has the "#100" box filled in, ignore the number;　it is only there for reference.

At the end of each Item, type *

Special cases

1.　If the "Delete" box is ticked, punch the "#100" box followed by

DELETE£ *

and ignore anything else which might appear on the form (and continuation forms, if any)

e.g.

#100 Item no.	LIBRARY COMPUTER FILE	Delete (tick)
D0753	UPDATING FORM	✓

would be punched

#100 D0753£ DELETE£ *

2.　Extra boxes might have been created on a form.

e.g.

#601 Author	#602
JONES G.	SMITH H.

would be punched

#601 JONES G.£ #602 SMITH H.£

B.2

e.g.

#8Ø1 Class	// #8Ø2 33Ø.4

would be punched

      #802 330.4£   (There is no #801)

The catalogued procedure (DLFPMCLG) used in Durham
University for the operation of the LFP System is shown in
figure C.1.   All of the sample jobs given in the book
make use of DLFPMCLG.   It consists of job control statements for four job steps labelled M,C,L and G.   We shall
describe the steps in turn.

(i)   Step M.   The Library File Program Generator
      (PGM=LFPG01) is executed.

      STEPLIB defines the program library containing
      LFPG01,

      SYSPL1 will contain the PL/1 program generated
      by LFPG01,

      SYSLIN is for Linkage Editor control statements
      generated by LFPG01.

      The user must supply a card file called SYSIN
      containing a program of commands.

(ii) Step C.   The PL/1(F) Compiler (PGM=IEMAA) is
      executed.

      SYSIN is the file containing the PL/1 program
      generated in step M,

      SYSLIN will contain the compiled program.

      The user need not normally override this step.

(iii) Step L.   The Linkage Editor (PGM=IEWL) is
      executed.

      SYSLIN contains both the compiled program from
      step C and the control statements from step M,

      SYSOBJ defines the library of LFP System programs
      (FINPUT, SORT, etc.),

      SYSLMOD will contain the complete program to obey
      the commands entered by the user in step M.

      The user need not normally override step L.

(iv) Step G.   The program which step L stored in file
      SYSLMOD is now executed.   The following files
      are defined and the user must supply any other

```
//M       EXEC PGM=LFPG01                                                      00000010
//STEPLIB DD DSN=LOAD.DUL01,UNIT=2314,VOL=SER=UNE040,DISP=SHR                   00000020
//SYSPRINT DD SYSOUT=A                                                         00000030
//SYSUT1  DD UNIT=2314,VOL=SER=UNE030,SPACE=(CYL,(1,1))                        00000040
//SYSPL1  DD UNIT=2314,VOL=SER=UNE999,SPACE=(CYL,(1,1)),DISP=(,PASS)           00000050
//SYSLIN  DD UNIT=2314,VOL=SER=UNE999,SPACE=(CYL,(1,1)),DISP=(,PASS)           00000060
//C       EXEC PGM=IEMAA,PARM='S,A,X,NT,NOL,NST',COND=(5,LT,M)                 00000070
//SYSPRINT DD DUMMY                                                           00000080
//SYSLIN  DD UNIT=2314,VOL=SER=UNE999,SPACE=(CYL,(1,1)),DISP=(,PASS)           00000090
//SYSUT1  DD UNIT=2314,VOL=SER=UNE999,SPACE=(CYL,(2,1))                        00000100
//SYSUT3  DD UNIT=2314,VOL=SER=UNE999,SPACE=(CYL,(2,1))                        00000110
//SYSIN   DD DSN=*.M.SYSPL1,DISP=(OLD,DELETE)                                  00000120
//L       EXEC PGM=IEWL,PARM='OVLY,LIST',COND=((5,LT,M),(5,LT,C))             00000130
//SYSPRINT DD DUMMY                                                           00000140
//SYSLIN  DD DSN=*.C.SYSLIN,DISP=(OLD,DELETE)                                  00000150
//        DD DSN=*.M.SYSLIN,DISP=(OLD,DELETE)                                  00000160
//SYSLIB  DD DSN=SYS1.PL1LIB,DISP=SHR                                          00000170
//SYSLMOD DD DSN=&G(MAIN),UNIT=2314,VOL=SER=UNE999,SPACE=(CYL,(1,1,2)),        00000180
//           DISP=(,PASS)                                                      00000190
//SYSOBJ  DD DSN=OBJ.DUL01,UNIT=2314,VOL=SER=UNE040,DISP=SHR                   00000200
//SYSUT1  DD UNIT=2314,VOL=SER=UNE999,SPACE=(CYL,(2,1))                        00000210
//G       EXEC PGM=*.L.SYSLMOD,COND=((5,LT,M),(5,LT,C),(5,LT,L))              00000220
//DUMMY   DD DUMMY                                                            00000230
//SYSPRINT DD SYSOUT=A                                                        00000240
//SYSCODE DD DSN=DUL01LCO,UNIT=2314,VOL=SER=UNE040,DISP=SHR,                   00000250
//           DCB=(RECFM=F,LRECL=66,DSORG=DA)                                   00000260
//WORK1   DD UNIT=2314,VOL=SER=UNE999,SPACE=(CYL,(5,1))                        00000270
```

Figure C.1   DLFPMCLG - Catalogued Procedure

file definitions required by his program.

DUMMY (see page 109 in Chapter 7),

SYSPRINT for printer output,

SYSCODE is an extant code translation file (see Chapter 8),

WORK1, for temporary working space, can be used either for card files or for internal files (but not both in the same job step) and will take up to 28,000 card records or 18,000 ("Durham-sized') internally formatted items.

This appendix describes one further LFP System feature and an IBM 360/OS facility which can be used to advantage, and discusses extensions to the system briefly.

D.1   *THE READ FACILITY*

In all of the descriptions of commands up to this point the parameters have been fixed before execution of the program of commands.   Suppose, for example, that we store the following program on a disk volume using program IMAGE (see the example at the end of section 9.4 and the next section of this appendix):

```
IN1 PROGRAM;
    FINPUT INDATA 80 ON NEW,BJPX,' ',ABCXY,'';
    END;
```

Whenever we use the program, we must define INDATA and NEW, on DD cards, as the input external file and the output internal file respectively.   Each time, all 80 columns of the cards (records) in INDATA must be used and a copy of the card file will always be printed.   The four one-character coded elements will be checked in the same way every time the program is used.

The READ facility enables us to postpone fixing the parameters until the program is actually executing - until the very last moment before they are required.   Thus we can, for example, write and store a program which will convert an external file, which is either numbered in columns 73-80 or not, to internal form, printing out the card file at our discretion.   The program is:

```
IN2 PROGRAM;
    FINPUT INDATA READ READ NEW,BJPX,' ',ABCXY,'',
    END;
```

The word READ, occurring in the place of a parameter in a command, instructs the computer to read the parameter from the special card file called CONTROL.   The reading is done immediately before the command is obeyed.   Suppose that IN2 is stored in the data-set DUL01IN2 and that we wish to convert an external file in which all 80 columns of the cards have been used for data and that no listing of the cards is required.   The following job will suffice:

```
//DUL01D1A JOB (0011,C105),LIBRARY
//      EXEC DLFPMCLG,TIME.G=(2,0)
//M.SYSIN DD DSN=DUL01IN2,UNIT=2314,VOL=SER=UNE040,DISP=SHR
//G.NEW DD DSN=DUL01NBK,UNIT=2314,VOL=SER=UNE110,
//       DISP=(NEW,KEEP),SPACE=(TRK,(20,2))
//G.INDATA DD *
  #100 D2317£ #300 A£ #401 PBX£ #500 1958£
```

            etcetera

```
/*
//G.CONTROL DD *
     80;        OFF;
/*
//
```

Rules for the use of READ

(i)   In the program of commands, READ may be used as many
      times as required in the place of file, string,
      number and switch types of parameter (see figure 7.1
      in chapter 7).   It may not be used to read in a
      routine name, a command label or a program name.   In
      the sample program IN2 above, READ is used for a
      number and a switch (in that order).   The restrictions
      on the use of READ make the following two commands
      illegal:

          SORT LBK OUT READ;
                         ^
                         should be a sequencing routine name

      LAB1 READ F33;
           ^
           should be a program name

      In the command

      READ UPDATE LBK AMEND LBK OFF;

      the word READ is interpreted as an ordinary label
      without special significance in the present context.

(ii) If READ occurs in a "goto" statement, it is taken
      to refer to a statement labelled "READ" - no reading
      is done.

(iii) READ occurring in a conditional (IF) statement
      always causes a read operation from file CONTROL.
      The program will expect to receive a number and
      will never use it as a label.

E.g.   The statement

       IF CHECK>READ;

compares the completion code set by the command
labelled CHECK with the number read from CONTROL.

(iv)   Whenever, during execution of the user's program,
the computer encounters the word READ in either
a conditional statement or a command in the position of a file name, string, number or switch, it
reads a new piece of data from file CONTROL. The
data must appear in file CONTROL in the order in
which it will be required by the executing program.

(v)   The data provided in file CONTROL must be of the
right type.   The symbol data stands for that
which is read in response to encountering one READ
during execution.   The correct syntax for data
in a particular case depends upon the type of
parameter which is required.   Figure D.1 gives
the various forms of data and, in the right hand
column, the assumptions which are made in the
event of syntax error.

(vi)   Comments, between /* and */, are permitted with
data and are equivalent to spaces, as usual.
The comma is also treated as a space.

(vii) File CONTROL may contain both data for READ's and
print-control statements.   Program PRINT starts
to read a set of print-control statements at the
beginning of a new card.

Similarly, if a statement or command in a program
requires any data from CONTROL, a new card will
be started (for the statement but not for each
READ in the statement).

175

Required parameter type	Syntax of data	Assumption in case of error
file name	FILE fname;	FILE DUMMY;
string	string;	''; – the empty string
number	number;	0; – zero
switch	ON OFF ⎬ ;	OFF;

Notes

fname is the name of a file properly defined in a DD statement.

string is any sequence of characters. To include space, comma, semicolon, enclose in quotes.

number is a whole number. Space and commas are not permitted within a number.

data must be terminated by a semicolon.

Spaces (or their equivalent) may occur before and after each component of data.

Figure D.1. Syntax of data for the READ facility

D.2   LIBRARIES OF SMALL CARD FILES

It is convenient to be able to store programs of commands and sets of print-control statements on a disk volume if they are to be used regularly. The most important reason for doing this is that the chance of error is reduced when we use proven cards without actually handling them every time.   The card files will normally be very short (10 cards or less) and it is wasteful to store each in a separate data-set, because the minimum allocation of space that can be made is 1 track and its capacity is 70 cards.

The IBM 360 operating system provides the facility for handling "partitioned" data-sets or "libraries".   Several files can be stored one after the other on the tracks of the disk volume with no gaps between them and a directory is kept (automatically) to indicate the location of each file within the data-set.   Figure D.2 is a map analogous to a partitioned data-set.   The files are stored in "members" of the library and each is individually accessible by specifying the data-set name and the member name.

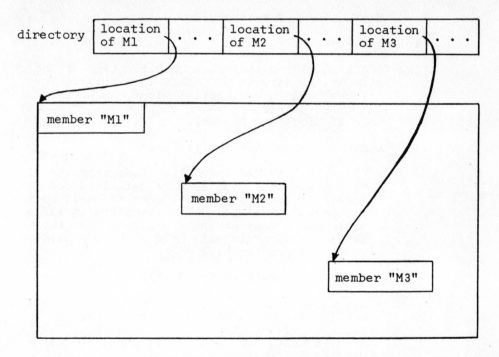

Figure D.2.   Map of a partitioned data-set containing (among others) members called M1, M2 and M3.

A partitioned data-set can be created at the same time as its first member in much the same way as an ordinary data-set for an internal or external file. The following DD statement parameters are required.

(i)   Data-set name (including the member name) written, for example, as follows:

DSN=DUL01LIB(PCORDER)

Member names, like data-set names, must have no more than 8 characters (letters and digits only allowed), the first of which must be a letter. Unlike data-set names, there is no necessity for further restriction on the choice of member names (on public disk volumes).

(ii)   UNIT=2314.   (Tapes cannot be used for partitioned data-sets.)

(iii) Volume.

        E.g.   VOL=SER=UNE040

(iv)   DISP=(NEW,KEEP).

(v)   SPACE must also include a specification of the size of the directory. This is expressed in "blocks" and in our case, 1 block can contain 21 member-entries. (A track of a 2314 disk can hold 17 directory blocks).

        E.g.   SPACE=(TRK,(5,1,10))

- allocate 5 tracks initially, increment the size by 1 track at a time as more data is added and create a directory of 10 blocks (to hold up to 210 member entries). The directory itself will occupy most of the first track, so the initial allocation will hold about 300 cards (70 cards per track).

        E.g.   SPACE=(TRK,(10,,5))

- allocate 10 tracks (no increment, so the data-set is of fixed size) and create 5 directory blocks. This data-set will hold up to 105 members containing a total of about 600 card-records.

The following job creates a partitioned data-set to hold small card files and stores the first member (called CSORT, it sorts a file into course/author order and prints an index and a list).

```
//DUL01D2A JOB (0010,C105),LIBRARY
//      EXEC DLFPMCLG
//M.SYSIN DD *
 STORE PROGRAM;
        IMAGE DATA 72 MEMBER ON;
        END;
/*
//G.MEMBER DD DSN=DUL01LIB(CSORT),UNIT=2314,VOL=SER=UNE040,
//     DISP=(NEW,KEEP),SPACE=(TRK,(5,1,15))
//G.DATA DD *
 PROGC PROGRAM;
        SORT MAIN COURSE SEQ467;
        COIND COURSE;
        PRINT CONTROL 72;
        END;
/*
//
```

Adding a new member to an existing partitioned data-set is done in the same way, but the DD statement defining the member must have DISP=OLD (the DISP parameter refers to the data-set, not the member) and need have no SPACE parameter.

If a file is written into a member which already has a card file in it, the latter is replaced by the new one.

Using a Member of a Partitioned Data-set

We illustrate the use of a partitioned data-set with a sample job. The program used is the one stored in member CSORT of data-set DUL01LIB in the job given above (DUL01D2A). File CONTROL contains a set of print-control statements to list the item numbers, authors and titles of all the items in a file called NEW. It then refers the program to file CTLG for further instructions. File CTLG is contained in another member (called PCCOURSE) of DUL01LIB and might, for example, produce a course/author catalogue (see file CONTROL in job DUL01EXA in section 7.5, chapter 7).

```
//DUL01D2B  JOB  (0005,C105,,6),LIBRARY,CLASS=C
/*HOLD ***  6000 LINES * * * CLASS C * * *
//STEPA  EXEC DLFPMCLG,TIME.G=(5,0)
//M.SYSIN DD DSN=DUL01LIB(CSORT),UNIT=2314,VOL=SER=UNE040,
//      DISP=SHR
//G.WORK2 DD UNIT=2314,VOL=SER=UNE020,SPACE=(TRK,(55,6))
//G.WORK3 DD UNIT=2314,VOL=SER=UNE030,SPACE=(TRK,(55,6))
//G.WORK4 DD UNIT=2314,VOL=SER=UNE040,SPACE=(TRK,(55,6))
//G.COURSE DD UNIT=2314,VOL=SER=UNE999,SPACE=(TRK,(73,7))
//G.MAIN DD DSN=DUL01LBK,UNIT=2314,VOL=SER=UNE040,DISP=SHR
//G.NEW DD DSN=DUL01A32,UNIT=2314,VOL=SER=UNE110,DISP=SHR
//G.CTLG DD DSN=DUL01LIB(PCCOURSE),UNIT=2314,VOL=SER=UNE040,
//      DISP=SHR
//G.CONTROL DD *
   LIST FILE NEW;
   5,(#100,4,#601), CONT IN 16, STOP IN 95;
   +4, TAB 40, #701, CONT IN 42, STOP IN 95;
   GO (CTLG);
/*
//
```

D.3   EXTENDING THE SYSTEM

Firstly it should be pointed out that the tasks of modifying and extending the LFP System belong to the programmer who will obtain technical information from the manual The Library File Processing System Computer Programs. The discussion here is simply to inform the reader of what can be done without drastic revision of the system. Modifications fall into two main categories, those that affect one or more commands and those that do not. We shall deal firstly with the latter because they are the easier to implement (that is not a comment on the programming, but on the incorporation of the new programs in the system).

(i) Simple replacement of LFP System programs

We would alter a program either because we can improve its efficiency or because we would like it to operate differently or because an error has been detected in the program. So long as the change in the program does not affect the types or number of the parameters used in the command to invoke it, there is normally nothing more to do than to replace it in the LFP System program library. A particular candidate for improvement in performance, for example, is the program SORT, and that can be done in isolation from the rest of the system. In a similar way it is possible to alter the service programs - routines that are used by the programs which we invoke in commands. For example, there is a routine for interpreting selection specifications and reading files accordingly, and the programs

180

FCOPY, PRINT and BATCH all use this same routine.
It might be decided that the present facility is
too restrictive and it would be a simple matter of
replacement in the program library once a new
selection routine had been written.

(ii)   Additional Programs

Under this heading, we deal with two types of
extension.   The first is the addition of a further
sequencing routine for use with the programs SORT,
MERGE and CHKSRT.   A name other than those given
in figure 5.1 (chapter 5) occurring in a command
will cause a warning message to be printed, but the
correct PL/1 program will be generated on the
assumption that the named sequencing routine will
be supplied by the user.

The second type of extension is the introduction
of a new command with its corresponding program.
In this case the program generator must be modified
before the command can be used.   The technical
manual explains how to change the program generator
so that it accepts new or modified commands.   One
might, for example, incorporate the programs
required for an ordering system.

1.   *PROGRAMS*

Program name	Function	Reference Section	Page
BATCH	Reads a card file containing externally formatted items and special instructions (BATCH and SELECT) for generating items and produces an external file suitable for conversion by program FINPUT.	9.3 9.2	142 137
CDLIST	Produces a listing of a card file.	9.5	149
CHKSRT	Examines an internally formatted file to see it is in a specified order.	5.4 5.1	57 49
CODEIN	Reads a card file containing information needed to decode certain of the coded elements and creates a code translation file for use by program PRINT.	8.2 8.1 6.2	130 121 71
COIND	Prints indices, in alphabetical order of codes and of translations, of the course codes (#401) occurring in an internal file.	8.3	133
FCOPY	Makes copies of items in an internal file. The copy may be selective.	4.3 4.4	41 44
FINPUT	Converts a file of bibliographic records from the external to the internal updating format.	4.1 3.4	31 26
FPUNCH	Converts a file of bibliographic records from the internal to the external format.	9.1	135

E

2. *COMMAND LANGUAGE*

Statement type	Function	Reference Section	Page
Conditional	Performs a comparison, the result of which determines which statement is obeyed next. The numbers compared are either given explicitly in the conditional statement or set on completion of previously executed commands in the program.	7.2 D.1	97 174
END	Marks the end of the pro-gram. When this statement is executed, the job step terminates.	7.2	102
GOTO	Instructs the computer to obey a specified statement next (instead of following the statements in sequence)	7.2	100
IF	(see "Conditional" above)		
PROGRAM	Obligatory first statement in a program of commands. May name the program.	7.2	97

3. *PRINT-CONTROL STATEMENTS*

Statement type	Function	Reference* Page
END	Indicates end of set of statements. After the print-ing, PRINT terminates. (See "execute").	80
execute	Instructs PRINT to execute the listing requested in the pre-ceding statements and specifies what is to be done next. END and GO are the execute state-ments.	80

---

*All details concerning print-control statements are in Section 6.2.

E

Statement type	Function	Reference Page
format	Specifies a text to be constructed of one or more elements and gives the layout on the printed page.	75 69
GO	An execute statement. After printing, program PRINT is to interpret another set of instructions in the file specified by the GO statement.	80
group heading	Identifies an element, the values of which are to be printed as headings above groups of items which have that element-value in common. LINE and PAGE statements are group heading statements.	73
HEADING	Inserts a line of text in each item that is printed.	78
LINE	A group heading statement. A new heading is printed on a new line.	73
LIST	Specifies the file(s) to be printed.	67
PAGE	A group heading statement. A new heading is printed at the top of a new page.	73
PRINT	(same as LIST, above)	
SELECT	Gives a selection specification (see Section 4.4) to be applied to all items read from the file(s) given in LIST or PRINT statements.	68
SKIP	Causes a new line to be started while formatting an item for printing. Blank lines can be included.	79
SPACE	Specifies the number of blank lines required between printed items.	69

In this appendix, check lists and charts are given to help the user to construct his computer jobs. Some of the detail is specific to the NUMAC installation at the time of writing and to the use of the catalogued procedure DLFPMCLG (see Appendix C), but the decisions to be taken by the user are typical. The assumption is that we have a program of commands, and we start by performing the following steps:

*   Make a list of all the files used in the program (including those not explicitly mentioned such as the work files for SORT) and note the type of each - card file or internal file.

*   Check that no file intended for punched card input is used more than once, either for input or output (note that CONTROL is exceptional in that it may be used for input several times).

*   Check that no file intended for punched card output is also used as an input file.

*   Estimate the number of items and cards (or 80-byte records) which will be processed by the various commands.

*   Hence, estimate the CPU time and disk storage requirements and work out the quantities of printed and punched output expected.

*   Against each file in the list, write down the disk volume (or device, if the file refers to the card reader or punch). For existing data-sets, the volumes are already determined and for new permanent data-sets, they are as arranged with the computer staff. Temporary files should be distributed on whichever volumes are usually available (current information on this subject is obtainable from the computing department).

*   Hence, make a list of volumes which will require to be mounted specially (e.g. private disk volumes).

We now have the information needed to punch the cards and to assemble a job. Chart F.1 is an aid to deciding the job class and chart F.2 tells the user where in the card deck to include information concerning the requirements of a job. Section 7.4 in Chapter 7 describes how a job is assembled; to recapitulate, the deck should contain cards in the following order:

*   The JOB card must come first (page 111).

*   If the job requires more than 10 minutes of CPU time or will print more than 3,000 lines or will punch more than 200 cards or requires a disk to be specially mounted, a HOLD card follows the JOB card (page 113).

*   The EXEC card comes next (page 112).

*   The program of commands is defined using a DD statement starting

//M.SYSIN DD

If the commands are on cards they follow now and are terminated by

/*

(pages 110 and 179)

*   If the printout for the G step is to be stored on a disk instead of being printed, include a DD statement beginning

//G.SYSPRINT DD

(page 150)

*   If the definition of file SYSCODE (the code translation file) in the catalogued procedure is not suitable, override it with a DD statement beginning

//G.SYSCODE DD

(page 132)

*   Include a DD statement for each file used except DUMMY, SYSCODE and WORK1. If a card file is to be read from the input stream containing the job, it follows the DD card and is terminated by

/*

*   The "end-of-job" card:

//

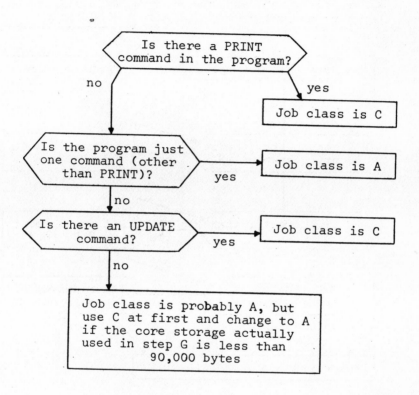

Chart F.1   Deciding the job class

F

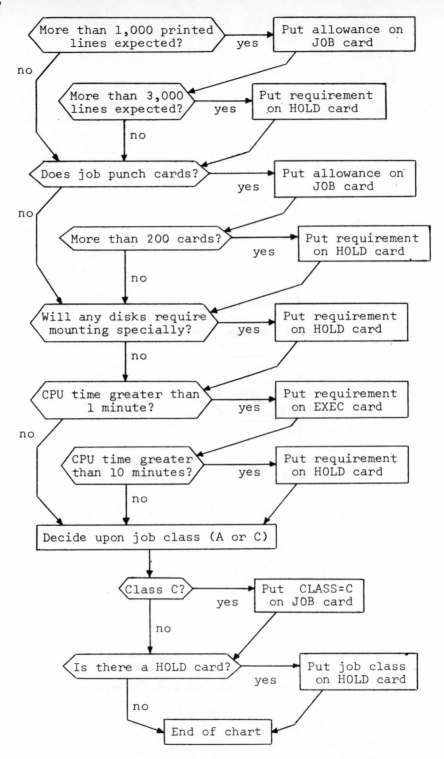

Chart F.2   Specifying the job's demands

For terms that are referred to more than once in the text, the primary reference is given first.

193

printed, output, 109,171
  price, 71
printer, 8,1
  stationery, 69,10,151
printing,
  card files, 149
  copies of print file, 151
  files, 61,2,9
    selectively, 68,61
  headings, 74
  instructions, 61
  orders, 144
  text composition, 73
printout,
  copies, 150
  large, 10
  limit, 111
  requirement, 187
private disk volume, 8,113
procedure, catalogued, see
  catalogued procedure
processing files, 2,12,21-4,
  89
  large, 10
PROG, 97
PROGRAM statement, 97,90,185
Program Generator, Library
  File, 93,12,169
program, see relevant name
  commands, 89-103,12,110,
    169
    storage, 147-8,7,177,179
  control, 11
  description, 13
  errors, correction, 180
  function, see relevant
    name
  label, 97
  "library", 12,2,16
  loading, 11
  name, 174
    EXEC statement, 16
    parameter, 95
programming language, 11
Programming Language One,
  see PL/1
programs, 13,2
  use, 3
protection of items in
  files, 38,35
prototype command, 13
public disk volume, 8
publication date, 27,1,164
publisher, 27,1,166

punched cards, 23,1,16,see
  card
  containing items, 22,161
  input, 187
  output, 187
    DD statement, 109
    limit, 111

Queue,
  job, 7
  output, 8

Range,
  element tags, 28
  elements, 50,71-2,164
  tags for print-control, 72·
READ, 173-6
  command label, 174
  conditional statement, 174
  data syntax, 176
  use,174
reader, card, 7
reading,
  files, 23
  parameter from CONTROL,
    173,175
  punched cards, 23
receipt date, 27,1,26,71,162
record, 21
  bibliographic, 21,see item
  identification, 1
recovery from failures, 91
reliability, 4
removal of elements, 39
replacement item number, 92
  internal format, 157
replacing,
  LFP System program, 180
  member of partitioned data-
    set, 179
report, agent's, 27,1
reproduction of files, see
  copying
re-reading card file, 63
resources, 5
  allocation, 5
  estimates, 114,116,118
  management, 11
  requirements, 8,113
    specification, 16
retention of data-set, 106
root,
  cards in code file, 129
  code tree, 122,126

stationery, printer,
69,10,151
status, 27,1,163
step, see job-step
storage,
  card file, 147
  disk, see disk
  files, 22,7
  high capacity, 7
  print file, 150
  print-control file,
    147-8,177
  program of commands,
    147-8,7,177,179
store, core, 7,11,112
stored,
  print-file DD statement,
    151
  print-control file, use,
    149
  programs, use, 149
string parameter, 94
string in print-control,
  65
structure of files, 21
subparameter in DD state-
  ment, 104
subprogram, 13
subroutine, 13
supervisor, 11
switch parameter, 95
symbolic name, 14
symbols,
  commands, 94
  print-control, 65
syntactic unit, print-
  control, 65-6
syntax,
  command, 95-6
    language, 94
  data for READ, 176
  external file, 29-30,138
  format statement, 75
  print-control statements,
    67
  selection specification,
    44
  text composition, 73
SYSCODE file, 121,63,71,188,
  see code translation file
  CODEIN, 131-2
  COIND, 133-4
  creation, 130
  DCB parameter, 108,131

SYSCODE file, definition, 171
  DLFPMCLG, 109
SYSIN file, input to LFPG01,
  110,169,188
SYSPRINT print file, 150-2,188
  definition, 171
system, LFP, see LFP System
  operating, see operating
  system

Tabulation, 77-8,86
tag, 21,26,29,138
temporary data-set, 107-8
terminating character in
  external item, 29
termination,
  job, 5,14,16,93
  PRINT, 81
test in selection specification,
  44
testing completion codes, 98,102
text,
  code tree, 124,126
  composition for printing, 73
three-character codes, 26,121
TIME, EXEC statement parameter,
  112,16
time, see CPU time
  elapse, 9
title, 27,1,164
  filing, 50,165
TODAY, 71-2
total copy, 42
track, disk volume, 7,106
  capacity for card file, 108
translation code, see code
  translation
tree, code, 121-5
type of publication, 27,1,162
types of information in item, 21

Underlined name, 14
union catalogue, 3
UNIT, DD statement keyword, 105
unselective copying, 42
UPDATE,
  command, 34
  completion codes, 40
  CPU time, 40
  DD cards, 39-40
  FINPUT with, 38
  program, 89
    function, 35-40,184
  use, 89-93